T0070083

THEE TRUTH

BONGA MAKHOLWA

authorHOUSE®

AuthorHouse™ UK
1663 Liberty Drive
Bloomington, IN 47403 USA
www.authorhouse.co.uk
Phone: 0800.197.4150

© 2015 Bonga Makholwa. All rights reserved.

No part of this book may be reproduced, stored in a retrieval system, or
transmitted by any means without the written permission of the author.

Published by AuthorHouse   06/09/2015

ISBN: 978-1-5049-4430-4 (sc)
ISBN: 978-1-5049-4429-8 (hc)
ISBN: 978-1-5049-4431-1 (e)

Print information available on the last page.

Any people depicted in stock imagery provided by Thinkstock are models,
and such images are being used for illustrative purposes only.
Certain stock imagery © Thinkstock.

This book is printed on acid-free paper.

Because of the dynamic nature of the Internet, any web addresses or links contained in
this book may have changed since publication and may no longer be valid. The views
expressed in this work are solely those of the author and do not necessarily reflect the
views of the publisher, and the publisher hereby disclaims any responsibility for them.

You awoke only to see that half the world was still asleep. You had the key to life but never came to understand that most of the time the questions are complicated and the answers are quite simple. For some time it had never hit you that you were looking far beyond that which actually is, when in fact all that you will ever need is lying still and deep inside of you, waiting for you to awaken.

The truth is, something within you is not in harmony with what you believe. Your will is just not in harmony with what should be. There is something within you that sees the world and knows that these "answers" are not leading to what actually should be.

All through life you have chosen to look at the world as you are and by what your circumstances told you. You never took time to look at it as it is and at its true nature. For I tell you the painful truth, life is really simple, but you insist on complicating it.

For I tell you the truth, as it is within, so it is without; as it is above, so it is below; as it is in heaven, so it is on earth; as it is with the Father, so it is with the Son; as it is with giving, so it is with receiving; as it is with sowing, so it is with reaping; as it is with thoughts, so it is with life.

The truth is as it is man within himself, so it is the world around him; as it is with the thoughts of man, so it is with the life of man; as it is with the Creator, so it is with His creations; as it is when a man gives, so it will be when he receives; as it is when man sows, so it is when he reaps; and as a man thinks, so will be his life.

For I tell the truth, man is what he thinks, not what he thinks he is. The truth is that man is created in the image of the Creator. The truth is that man is ever creating as the Creator is always creating. The truth is that man is the result of his thoughts and actions. The truth is that man does not live on food alone, but by every word that he speaks from his heart that leaves his mouth.

For the truth is everything comes from everything, and everything is made up of everything, and so everything returns to everything.

For whoever has ears, do not just hear but listen; for whoever has eyes, do not just see but perceive; for whoever has a heart, do not just feel but understand.

For I tell you the truth, you are a spiritual being on a human being's journey and not a human being on a spiritual journey. You are part of a whole, called by you the "universe" or the "world," which is limited by time and space. You experience yourself, your thoughts and your feelings as something "separate" from the rest of the universe. This illusion of consciousness has led you to attempt to enter the kingdom of God through the wide gate.

For I tell you the truth, the truth that you already know. The truth is there is only one God, and that one God does not have a religion. There is only one God, and that one God does not have a tradition. There is only one God, and that one God does not have a gender. There is only one God, and that one God lives inside each and every single person and living thing.

For some time it had never hit you. Though you were seeing, you never actually perceived. Though you were hearing, you never actually listened. Though you were feeling, you never actually understood.

For I tell you the truth, God has given you a mind that even when your eyes are closed can see the past that has happened, the present that is happening, and the future that is going to happen. For everything you have done, are doing, or are going to do has got to start within your mind. For with your mind you create everything around you. You are what you think, not what you think you are. Think about it – now think about it.

For I tell you the truth, God has given you a heart that even when untouched, can feel the past you have been through, the present that you are going through, and the future you are going to go through.

2

The truth is all that completes us is how we feel. The feelings of love, freedom, and peace are felt from within the heart. For you know that the most beautiful things in life are not seen but are felt by the heart.

For I tell you the truth, you were made in God's exact image; you were made in His exact likeness; you were made to create just like Him. You have a brain in your head and you have feet in your shoes. You can steer yourself in any direction you choose.

The truth is you are what you think, not what you think you are. For your whole life has been made up of what you have thought. For every thought there was an action. For every action there was a consequence. And in all that we called it life.

For I tell you the truth. Take a look at the world closely. Now see what I see, feel what I feel, understand what I understand, and perceive what I perceive.

You see that the one who talks the most about sickness is the one who experiences sicknesses the most. The one who talks the most about wealth and prosperity is the one who experiences the most wealth and prosperity in his life. The one who talks the most about poverty and not having enough is the one who experiences poverty and at most times does not have enough to get by. The one who talks the most about fear is the one who lives his life in fear. The one who talks the most about happiness is the one who lives his life in happiness.

For I tell you the truth. Again I say to you, you are made in the exact image of God. Every thought you dwell on and every word that comes out of your mouth will be your life.

For the truth is man does not live on bread alone but on every word that comes from the mouth of God.

For I tell the truth, everything that comes into your life, you bring to yourself by the images and feelings you hold in your head. Whether you are thinking about the past, the present, or the future, you are the exact image of God, and so you are creating the life around you as you think.

3

The truth is you mistake the world on two accounts:
that it is still and that it is comprised of things.

For everything is made up of the exact same thing. Everything
in the world is made up of energy, and through energy is where
God reveals himself. For everything comes from everything, and
everything is made up of everything, and so everything returns to
everything. For energy can never be created nor can it be destroyed.
It always was and has been. It moves into form, through form,
and out of form. For God always was and has been. He can never
be created nor be destroyed. He is all that ever was and will be.
He is always moving to form, through form, and out of form.

The truth is God is not sitting in the sky watching the earth
from a distant view, nor does He depend on chance. What you
perceive as physical is the direct reflection of what is invisible
but knowable. For just as love is perceived in a physical form
but is a direct reflection of what is invisible but also knowable,
in the same way, God presents Himself in this presence.

For you are a spiritual being and not a human being. For
you are energy and not a body. For you are that which you
call God. For you are made in His exact likeness.

Since the beginning of time, the Creator gave his creations the power
to rule over the earth. The gift of having free will is that which
gives the creations power to choose any path that may unfold.

For in life you see that day by day nothing seems to change, but when
you look back, you are often amazed at how much things have changed.

Life is a constant journey that unfolds right before our very
eyes just as it has been unfolding right inside our minds.

We mistake the Creator as a man who plays dice. The delusions of
what we have been told have led us to think that what happens to us
in life is a result of the Creator rather than that of us, His creations.

The truth is when the Creator was done with creation, he gave
his creations power to live freely and the will to choose.

For what you are is the gift God gave you, and so what
you will become will be your gift to God.

Though ever present in his creations, the Creator gives his creations
the power to create whatever they choose to create. He grants his
creations' wishes as they continue to unfold in thought, feeling,
word, and deed. Like a mirror he reflects what is created.

"For I will never forsake nor leave you; wherever you go I will
be there; whenever you are asleep I will be there. For wherever
my creations are, I will also be there, just as in the beginning
I was there, so till the end I will always be there."

For I tell you the truth, you have been given this life, and only you can
live this life of yours. Only you can be the greatest you can be; only
you are responsible for you; and at the end of the journey of life, only
you will be held liable for the life you have lived – no one else but you.

For the Creator grants his creations anything they choose.
For God is like a mirror in your life. Whatever you see in the
inside will be revealed on the outside. For every thought, word,
deed, and action, God – like the mirror he is – will reflect
everything in your eyes what you will perceive as life.

For long you may have viewed yourself as having no say in what
happens in your life or even life itself. For long you have limited
your chance to mirror back anything you want in your life by
giving exactly what you want in thought, word, deed, or action.

For long you thought there as a difference between the love you
give to your family and the love you give to a stranger. Every person
you meet is a person to be loved. The warm, full hug you give a
family member has the same measure as the warm hug needed by a
stranger that you deny. The good thoughts you have of loved ones
have the same measure as the thoughts you have of any person.

Every person is a reflection of you, but the illusions of the world have clouded the view. We are building too many walls and not many bridges. We distance ourselves from each other out of fear. We restrict ourselves to our personal desires and to affection for a few people nearest to us. The chase for money has left people broke of love.

For you have been led astray. Your focus was on what you thought were the big things, though they turned out to be ashes.

For too long you were seeing but not perceiving, feeling but not understanding. Now I want you to see with your mind, I want you to feel with your heart.

About two thousand years ago, the Son of man graced the earth with a mission and a purpose – a mission and purpose most people have dearly misunderstood or at least have been led to think that what is is actually what is.

For at the time the Son of man graced this earth, there were people of power; there were people who wanted control over others; there were people who wanted everything for themselves; there were people who wanted to represent the bad; there were people who chose greed, hate, and jealousy.

The truth is today nations are divided against other nations, people are divided against each other and differentiated by their beliefs. The illusion of the value of status and money has people confused. The blind are leading the masses in a world where you have to convince people that it is wrong to hurt innocent children. This world echoes the past. For I tell you the truth, the Creator knew that his creations would go astray at some point in their journey and forget the true purpose of creation, whether four thousand years ago, two thousand years ago, the years we are in, or the next century to come.

So to bring his creations back into the light, the Creator created the Son of man – but for a purpose many people have misunderstood.

The Son of man was created in order to bring all creations back to the path of light. He brought teachings to help the creations. He uttered in parables things hidden since the creation of time. He was an example of what the Creator wanted from his creations. He was what the Creator created and wanted his creations to be. He created the Son of man as the benchmark.

"Anyone who wants to go to the Father must go through me." For anyone who wants to see the Creator has to become like the Son of man, not merely "accept" him as Lord and Saviour.

Many people have misunderstood the purpose of the Son of man. Many have thought the Son of man was created as a sacrifice to die for their sins. Many have thought the Son of man graced the earth to seek praise and worship. Many have thought the Son of man graced this earth to be served for eternity. Many have thought the Son of man graced this earth to start a religion or a following.

This delusion has caused many people to try to enter the kingdom of God through the wide gate rather than the narrow gate.

When I see the world I remember the words "These people honour me with their words, but their deeds and hearts are far away from me".

So then, how has the world repeated history when the light of the world had shone on it? I tell you the truth, you have remembered the man and forgotten the message. You have been listening to what others had to say about the Son of man and not what the Son of man said.

Let us take a step back and see not where we fell but where we tripped.

For the same people who killed the Son of man, the same people who denied ever knowing the Son of man, the same people who mocked the Son of man went on to be part of the writing in the book that was soon to be known as the book of truth.

For I tell you the truth, if your mind and heart are filled with greed, hate, jealousy, prejudice, secrecy, and violence, the result will always be death, lack, hate, greed, and prejudice.

This is the result of us and the world.

For how likely were they to have a sudden change of heart? How likely were they to contribute true teachings? How likely were they to try and save themselves by dragging along billions of people with them? How likely were they to continue their evildoing to withhold their places of honour given by men? How likely were they to lead people astray?

A good tree does not bear bad fruit, nor will a bad tree bear good fruit. The world is the result of what we have made it. How has the world borne such bad fruit when it had such a good tree to pick from?

For I tell you the truth, the world is the opposite of what the Son said it should be, for the world has only remembered the man and has forgotten the message. The constant cycle of chasing money and success with all your mind, heart, and soul has led you to lose the race to the Creator of loving him with all your mind, heart, and soul. You are caught in the delusion of loving those closest to you with all your mind, heart, and soul. You lost sight of loving your neighbour with all your mind, heart, and soul, trapped in the idea of religion while knowing that God does not have a religion.

For I tell you the truth, when the Son of man was said to save people from sin, it did not mean that the sins of people will be no more. For when you save someone from sin, you show that person how to proceed with life – a life of no sin. Then the person will embark on life attempting what you have taught them.

For I tell you the truth, when the Son of man graced this earth, he didn't grace it as a sacrifice of eternity for people. For he graced the earth to be an example of what it takes for a person to be in the kingdom of God.

For people have been led to think that the Son of man graced this earth to die for their sins and wrongdoing. People have been led to think the Son of man graced this earth to start a religion. People have been led to think the Son of man graced this earth to be praised for eternity. People have been led to remember the name of the man and have forsaken the message.

For I tell you the truth, the Son of man graced this earth to live and be the light for others. The Son of man graced this earth to enlighten and show people the way. The Son of man graced this earth to be an example of what God wants us to be like. The Son of man graced this earth to show you the way to God, the way to love, the way to hope, the way to peace, the way to the kingdom of heaven.

For I tell you the truth, out of all the time that the Son man graced this earth, all he ever did was to serve the people, and not once did he want to be served like a king or even a god. Then why are you painting him as if he needs daily praise?

In all the time that the Son of man graced this earth, never did he go around telling people that he was going to die for them and that they needed to accept him as Lord and spend the rest of their lives singing praises to him. Then why do you live your life sinning, thinking someone has erased your wrongdoing?

In all the time that the Son of man graced this earth, never did he once tell those he met and taught that he came here to start a religion, and that they should build places of worship for him. Then why do you think you will find God in a religion or place of worship?

For I tell you the truth, it is quite obvious that people are doing the opposite of what the Son of man told them to do, or at least have been led to think that the path they are on is the right one.

For we have painted God to be this giant man who lives in the sky, who wants human praise, who destroys and creates people's lives, who loves the select few. But I tell you the truth, God is a comedian performing for a crowd who are afraid to laugh.

For I tell you the truth, as it was before the time the Son of man graced this earth, so it is now in the times we live in: a world divided by religions, a world divided by races, a world divided by beliefs, a world divided by borders, a world divided by human status, a world divided in its own world.

For the Son of man graced this earth when the times were just like present times. For if God loved the world so much that he gave up his Son, He wouldn't give him up in vain just so that a few years later a cycle of sinning, hate, and division would again come to pass, just like before he graced the earth.

For I tell you the truth, you have been given one life. Only you can live this life of yours; only you can walk the path which you please to go; only you can determine the destiny of your life; only you can be you; only you can answer for the life you live; only you have the chance to be you; and so only you can die for you.

For at the end of your life, all that will matter will be how you lived your life, how much love you gave, how much happiness you gave, how much hope you gave, and how much good you created with the power given to you.

For at the end of our lives, what will matter will not be the amount of money we made, how many degrees and diplomas we gained, the number of times we went to church, the jobs we had, the material objects we own, or the number of times we say "Lord, Lord".

There will come a time when you will have to answer for your life. For I tell the truth, no one can say "the Son of man died for me". For the question will again arise: What did you with the life you were given? For I tell you the truth, if you did not produce good fruits from your life, the Son of man will say to you "Go away from me. I don't know you."

Something within you senses that not all that are you being told is true. A voice inside you has been fighting a battle against the world which tries its utmost day and night to make you somebody else.

For a long time, you have listened to the voices outside you and have ignored the voice inside you. For a long time, the outer opinions seemed to be louder than the inner voice.

For a long time, you have listened to what people had to say about the Son of man and not to what the Son of man said.

For we were told to "love your God with all your mind, with all your heart, and with all your soul," and also to "love your neighbour as you would love yourself".

But I tell you the truth, from Monday, Tuesday, Wednesday, Thursday, Friday, Saturday, and Sunday you live your life trying by all means with all your heart, with all your mind, and with all your soul to finally have enough money so you can be happy and free and do anything you want to do without having any worries.

For I tell you the truth, you love your family, close friends, and those who can contribute something towards you. You have no time for strangers who waste your time with meaningless conversations or for small talk that leads nowhere. When you meet the opposite sex, all you see is potential spouses or ones that cannot even be considered to be part of your future.

For I tell you the truth, you will continue this cycle of events and interactions until you reach old age. Is that what life is about?

I don't think so.

Now is the time to remember the message and not just the man.

Just as the Creator brought us His cherished Son, the Son brought along all that we needed in our path, for he uttered parables that had been hidden since the time of creation.

Let's take a step back and remember the message.

SALT AND LIGHT

You are the salt of the earth, but if the salt loses its saltiness, how can it be made salty again? It is no longer good for anything, except to be thrown out and trampled by men.

You are the light of the world. A city on a hill cannot be hidden, neither do people light a lamp and put it under a bowl. Instead they put it on its stand and it gives light to everyone in the house. In the same way, let your light shine before men, that they may see your good deeds and praise your Father in heaven. – Matthew 5:13–16

You are a creation that creates. You are the essence of love. You are the light of the world. You are the centre of creation. You are made to love, and if you lose the love in your heart, what then are you good for except to be trampled and controlled by men who determine when and what you do in life? You are ruled more by the rules made by men that have ignored the commandments given to you by the Creator. Every day your day-to-day purpose is to fulfil the desires of this world as the chase of money would have you doing.

You are the light created to ignite other lights. You are made to be greatest you can possibly be. You are made to be a shining example of the Creator. You are made to prosper and have abundance. You are the light of the world.

Why then do you spend your time trying to change who you are and the creation you were made to be? It seems you have forgotten the special gift you are, being so distracted, trying to be like someone or something you are not and trying to fit in when you were born to

stand out. You are the light that is meant to shine, but you cannot
be a light that shines while trying to be something you're not.

You were made whole, and nothing more needs to be added to you.
You have everything that you need inside you. You are the creation
that creates. Now let your light shine in the world. Let the love inside
you fill the world. Let the world see the example of the Creator.

The light inside you is the love you were gifted with since you were in
your mother's womb. Let your life be full of so much love that others
see your good deeds and therefore see the light of the Creator. Let
your life be a shining example to others like the Son of man's was.

Never let the light of the love inside you be diminished
in any way. For I tell you the truth, once you lose the love
inside you, you lose your soul. Once you lose your soul, you
will be no more than a mat for men to trample on.

For I tell you the truth, the body goes to the earth, belongings
go to other people, and the soul goes to God.

Never lose the light of love inside you while trying to
pursue the things that go to the earth and the people.

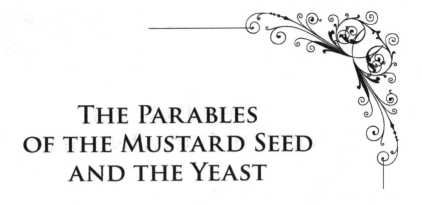

THE PARABLES
OF THE MUSTARD SEED
AND THE YEAST

The kingdom of heaven is like a mustard seed, which a man took and planted in his field. Though it is the smallest of all your seeds, yet when it grows, it is the largest of garden plants and becomes a tree, so that the birds of the air come and perch in its branches.

The kingdom of heaven is like yeast that a woman took and mixed into a large amount of flour until it worked all through the dough.

I will open my mouth in parables, I will utter things hidden since the creation of the world.

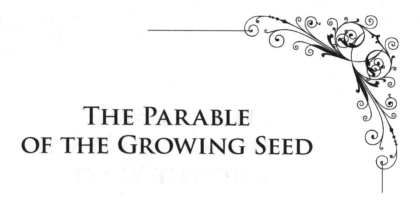

THE PARABLE
OF THE GROWING SEED

The kingdom of God is like a farmer who scatters seed on the
ground. Night and day, whether he is asleep or awake, the seed
sprouts and grows, but he does not understand how it happens.
Earth produces the crops on its own. First a leaf blade pushes
through, then the heads of wheat are formed, and finally the
grain ripens. As soon as the grain is ready, the farmer comes
and harvests it with a sickle, for the harvest time has come.

For I tell you the truth, you are made to have abundance. Your
life is like the yeast mixed in the flour, ever increasing what is in
its presence. For whatever you hold in heart and in thought will
increase until it is manifested in your life. For just as the mustard
seed is the smallest of seeds, so your thoughts are small. But
when the mustard seed grows, it becomes the largest plant and
becomes a tree. So it will be with your thoughts. As your thoughts
continue, soon you are amazed at the time they pass us as life.

For I tell you the truth, the Creator has given you all that you
could possibly ever need. All that you must do is create and He
will create more. You have been given the gift of life. No one can
walk the path ahead for you. You have love in you heart; you
have feet in your shoes; you have a mind in your head; you have
the Creator ever present; you have everything that you need.

For the truth is you have everything you will ever need and require
inside you. For the Creator who lives inside you will always multiply
and give in abundance whatever you bring forth in your soul.

THE PARABLE
OF THE TALENTS

Again, it will be like a man going on a journey, who called his servants and entrusted his property to them. To one he gave five talents of money, to another two talents, and to another one talent, each according to his ability. Then he went on his journey. The man who had received the five talents went at once and put his money to work and gained five more. So also, the one with two talents gained two more. But the man who had received the one talent went off, dug a hole in the ground and hid his master's money.

After a long time the master of those servants returned and settled accounts. He called the servant who had received the five talents. "Master," he said, "you entrusted me with five talents. See, I have gained five more."

His master replied, "Well done, good and faithful servant! You have been faithful with a few things, I will put you in charge of many things. Come and share your master's happiness!"

The man with the two talents also came. "Master," he said, "you entrusted me with two talents. See, I have gained two more."

His master replied, "Well done, good and faithful servant! You have been faithful with a few things, I will put you in charge of many things. Come and share your master's happiness!"

Then the man who had received the one talent came. "Master," he said, "I knew that you are a hard man, harvesting where you have not sown and gathering where you have not scattered seed. So I was afraid and went out and hid your talent in the ground. See, here is what belongs to you."

His master replied, "You wicked, lazy servant! So you knew that I harvest where I have not sown and gather where I have not scattered seed? Well then, you should have put my money on deposit with the bankers, so that when I returned I would have received it back with interest.

"Take the talent from him and give it to the one who has the ten talents. For everyone who has will be given more, and he will have an abundance. Whoever does not have, even what he has will be taken from him. And throw that worthless servant outside, into the darkness, where there will be weeping and gnashing of teeth."

For I tell you the truth, just as the servants each received talents
that the master had entrusted them with, so has the Creator
given you talents and love that he has entrusted to you. For you
have been given this life, and only you can live it. Only you are
entrusted with it. Only you can fulfil the purpose of your life.

For at the beginning of your life you were given the love that was
instilled in you. For you have been entrusted by the Creator to
take the love he has given you and multiply it. For you have been
entrusted to give your love to the deserving and the undeserving.
For just as the Creator sends rain to the righteous and unrighteous,
you too are expected to spread the seeds of the love within
yourself everywhere you go. For you have been trusted that in
the end the love that was given will come back with interest.

The truth is at the end of your life, the Creator will require
back what he has entrusted you with. For at the beginning
of your life, he entrusted you with all the love you need.

The question that remains is whether you will be the servant that takes what he has been given and increases it in abundance, or will you be the servant that hides what he has been given and does not increase it.

Will you, at the end of you life, have loved the Creator and
your neighbour with all your heart, with all your soul, and
with all your mind as you would like to be loved?

Will you, at the end of your life, have loved money and a select few
people with all you heart, with all your soul, and with all your mind?

Will you have taken the love you have been given
and have given it in abundance, or will you have kept
it in you, hidden for only the select few?

At the end of our lives, there will be two gates to
enter: the narrow gate and wide gate.

For I tell you the truth, there is only one way to enter through
the narrow gate to the Creator. That way is the way of love;
that is the way of righteousness; that is the way of peace;
that is the way of unity; that is the way of faith; that is the
way of the Son of man; that is the way of the Creator.

For I tell you the truth, there are many ways to enter through
the wide gate to the path of destruction. It is the way of the
pursuit of money; it is the way of violence; it is the way of politics;
it is the way of material things; it is the way of religions; it is
the way of the world. And that gate leads to destruction.

For to those who keep their love and give it only to their loved ones,
and to those who seem to think the master harvests where he has
not planted and have decided to keep their love in their homes like
the servant who hid his talent, I tell you – while you still have a
chance, increase the love you have been entrusted with, so you can
also enjoy the happiness of your Creator. Let your life not be of the
servant who hid his talent and therefore was sent to the eternal fire.

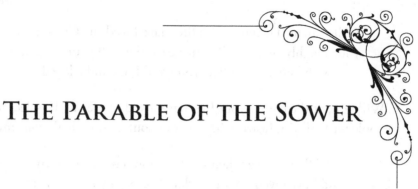

THE PARABLE OF THE SOWER

A farmer went out to sow his seed. As he was scattering the seed, some fell along the path, and the birds came ate it up. Some fell on rocky places, where it did not have much soil. It sprung up quickly, because the soil was shallow. But when the sun came up, the plants were scorched, and they withered because they had no root. Other seed fell among thorns, which grew up and choked the plants. Still other seed fell on good soil, where it produced a crop – a hundred, sixty, or thirty times what was sown. He who has ears, let him hear.

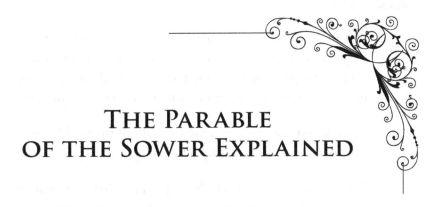

THE PARABLE
OF THE SOWER EXPLAINED

When anyone hears the message about the kingdom and does not understand it, the evil one comes and snatches away what was sown in his heart. This is the seed sown along the path. The one who received the seed that fell on rocky places is the man who hears the word and at once receives it with joy. But since he has no root, he lasts only a short time. When trouble or persecution comes because of the word, he quickly falls away. The one who received the seed that fell among the thorns is the man who hears, but the worries of this life and the deceitfulness of wealth choke it, making it unfruitful. But the one who received the seed that fell on good soil is the man who hears the word and understands it. He produces a crop, yielding a hundred, sixty, or thirty times what was sown.

For just as there were four types of seed that fell along their different paths, so we see people that have fallen in different ways in life.

For the seed sown along the path represents people who don't understand the message of the kingdom of God. The masses are doing the opposite of what the Son of man said they must do. Forgetting the message of love in their hearts, the evils of the world snatch the love that was sown in their hearts and so become like the seed that was sown along the path.

For the seed that fell on rocky places means the people who hear the message of the kingdom of God and seem to grasp the message for a short time. But when troubles and the world persecute them for being righteous, they fall away and go with the crowd.

The seed that is choked by the thorns

For I tell the truth, you are made to prosper; you are made to create; you are made to have abundance; you are made to love. But if you lose your inner self of love, abundance, and prosperity, you may as well be a mat for men to trample on.

For I tell you the truth, you are the light of the world; you are made to shine; you are made to be the light that ignites others.

For the world is trying endlessly to determine what you do and who you are. You are continuously living backwards. You are constantly in stress over what it may have in store for you. You are constantly living up to the demands of the world. You are constantly in a corner, available to love only a few.

For you have deserted your one true gift to create, your one true gift to create love, your one gift to create happiness, your one true gift to create hope, your one true gift to create abundance, your one true gift to be the light that ignites others to shine as brightly as possible.

For I tell you the truth, in life you determine who you are. The world cannot determine you. You are a creator that creates that which you wish to experience. You are the light that creates good. And in doing so, that light ignites other lights along its path. For when one lights another one's path, he brightens his path, too.

For you were not made to fit. You were made to stand out. For you are the light of the world. For you have a mind in your head. With your thoughts you can steer any direction you choose to go. You have feet in your shoes. With your heart you have the greatest director of your life. Right now you have the power to create the greatest good, like your Father in heaven. You have the power to create love everywhere you go. You have the power to create abundance with every good word you speak.

For when you become the light of the world, like your Father in heaven, you will ignite the world around you. The light you give off will come back like a boomerang, bringing more light.

For you can choose to be the light and shine upon darkness, bringing light to everywhere you go, or to be the darkness and to be the inferior of light, being shone upon and having others determine the circumstance.

For if you have ears, do not just hear, but understand. Do not be the seed that fell along the path and went on to move with the crowd only to end up no further than the crowd. And do not be the seed that fell on the rocky places and because of the fears and troubles of this world found itself in pieces. And do not be the seed that fell on thorns and have the delusions of wealth and material things turn it into dust. Rather be the seed that fell on good soil and produced a hundred of what was sown by increasing what was given to you – which is love.

THE FULFILMENT
OF THE LAW

Do not think I have come to abolish the Law or the Prophets. I have not come to abolish them but to fulfil them. I tell you the truth, until heaven and earth disappear, not the smallest letter, not the least stroke of pen, will by any means disappear from the Law until everything is accomplished. Anyone who breaks one of the least of these commandments and teaches others to do the same will be called least in the kingdom of heaven, but whoever practices and teaches these commands will be called great in the kingdom of heaven. For I tell you that unless your righteousness surpasses that of the Pharisees and the teachers of the law, you will certainly not enter the kingdom of heaven.

For I tell you the truth, many if not all of humanity have mistaken the purpose of the Son of man. People have thought the Son of man came as a sacrifice to die for people's sins and to become Lord in the afterlife. The Son of man actually came to fulfil the writings of prophets like the righteous Moses. Humanity thought the commandments handed to them were nearly impossible for a human to follow. The Son of man came to earth to fulfil these commandments and to be an example to other humans, showing that the commandments can be obeyed with ease if one walks with faith in God at every turn.

For I tell you the truth, humanity till this day has chosen to take the easy path instead of the right path. We choose what is easy every time and then ignore what is right.

The truth was hidden for centuries but remained after everything else changed or perished, even after all of humanity moved away from the will of God. For humanity has ignored the commandments given to them, and people have taught each other to conform to the rules designed and given by men. How then are we not to be called least in the kingdom of heaven?

Instead of seeking the kingdom of God first and therefore loving him and his creations with all our hearts, with all our minds, and with all our souls, we have moved in the opposite direction. We have sought the kingdom of earth first and therefore have our sights set on and are dedicated to money, with all our minds, with all our hearts, and with all our souls.

We have taught our children to become men and women who aspire to get rich, to accumulate as much money as they can. And we call that "education".

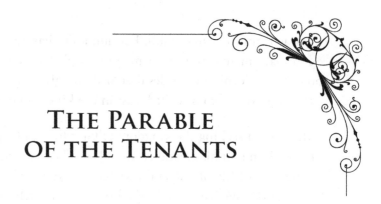

THE PARABLE
OF THE TENANTS

There was a landowner who planted a vineyard. He put a wall around it, dug a winepress in it, and built a watchtower. Then he rented the vineyard to some farmers and went away on a journey. When the harvest time approached, he sent his servants to the tenants to collect his fruit.

The tenants seized his servants. They beat one, killed another, and stoned a third. Then he sent other servants to them, more than the first time, and the tenants treated them the same way. Last of all, he sent his Son to them. "They will respect my Son," he said.

But when the tenants saw the Son, they said to each other, "This is the heir. Come, let us kill him and take his inheritance." So they took him and threw him out of the vineyard and killed him. Therefore when the owner of the vineyard comes, what will he do to those tenants?' "He will bring those wretches to a wretched end," they replied, "and he will rent the vineyard to other tenants, who will give him his share of the crop at harvest time."

The Son of man replied to them, "Have you never read in the Scriptures

'the stone the builders rejected has become the capstone, the Lord has done this, and it is marvellous in our eyes?'"

> For I tell you the truth, I tell you what I tell you not
> to change your beliefs. I tell you what I tell you not to
> change who you are, but to reveal the truth to you.

For too long the truth remained hidden. We have searched for it in the wrong places. We have searched outside ourselves, not knowing that he who looks outside dreams but he who looks within awakens.

For we have set our sights on the outside for money and have forgotten the love that is within. For we have devoted our minds, hearts, and souls to money and have forgotten the kingdom of God that moths cannot destroy and thieves cannot steal.

The moment we chose to devote our lives to making money is the moment we chose to give our energy and time to a piece of paper that cripples the time to create love, abundance, and joy. For time is the biggest gift. And you choose to devote it to money?

The moment we chose to devote our love to only the select few who are closest to us is the moment we chose to limit our love, abundance, and peace to a few. For the love in your heart is the greatest gift you can give to anyone. And you choose to devote it to a select few?

For I tell you the truth, we are certainly called least in the kingdom of heaven if we devote our time and love to money and a few people.

But I tell you the truth, whoever practices the commandments of love will be called great in the kingdom of heaven.

For whoever practices love for God and his creations will reap love from God and his creations. For whoever practices love for others will reap the love of others. For whoever creates abundance for others, creates abundance for oneself. For whoever creates happiness for others, creates happiness for oneself.

For I tell you the truth, if your righteousness does not surpass that of a child, then you cannot enter the kingdom of heaven. If your love does not surpass that of a child, then you cannot receive the love you truly deserve. If you have guilt, hate, jealousy, and worry in your heart, you cannot expect your life to be filled with peace, love, abundance, and hope.

MURDER

You have that it was said to the people long ago, "Do not murder, and anyone who murders will be subject to judgment." But I tell you that anyone who is angry with his brother without cause will be subject to judgment. Again any one who says to his brother "Raca" is answerable to the Sanhedrin. But anyone who says "You fool!" will be in danger of the fire of hell.

Therefore, if you are offering your gift at the altar and there remember that your brother has something against you, leave your gift there in front of the altar. First go and be reconciled to your brother, then come and offer your gift.

Settle matters quickly with your adversary who is taking you to court. Do it while you are still together with him on the way, or he may hand you over to the officer, and you may be thrown into prison. I tell you the truth, you will not get out until you have paid the last penny.

For I tell you the truth, to be angry with a person is like drinking poison and expecting the other person to die. For every bad thought and feeling you have towards a person will return to you as an action with the same measure. For everything we proclaim with our minds, souls, hearts, and words returns to us like the dog that goes back to its vomit.

For we must seek to make all our relationships with people good. We must seek to send out love even if there is hate. We must seek to send out reconciliation even if there is a feud. We must seek to send out peace, even if there was war. We must seek to create, even if there was destruction.

For if we choose to keep hate, the hate will affect us and only us, for our lives will be full of hate. If we choose to keep feuds, our lives will produce only feuds. If we choose to keep war, our lives will produce war all around us. And if we choose to keep the destruction, our lives will be filled only with destruction.

For I tell you the truth, the very weakness of violence is that it is a downward spiral. For it will continue to increase and multiply the very thing that it fights and seeks to destroy.

Instead of diminishing and removing evil, it multiplies it more than it was before. For whatever you send out in thought, word, and deed always comes back to you multiplied with more than before.

For I tell you the truth, though you may murder the liar through violence, you cannot murder the lie, nor can you ever establish the truth. The liar may not be there anymore, but the lie will remain forever.

For I tell you the truth, though you may murder the hater through violence, you certainly cannot murder the hate nor establish any love. For the hater may be no more, but the hate will remain forever.

For the truth is violence will always create more violence and even more hate, and so on and on. For returning violence with more violence will create more violence, thus adding more darkness in a world that is already full of violence and darkness. For darkness cannot drive out darkness; only light can do that. And so hate cannot drive out hate; only love can do that.

For if we all returned violence with violence, how would we survive in this world? How would we be different from the evildoers who do everything they do in the name of violence?

For in the end, it will never be between you and people but between you and God.

ADULTERY

You have heard it was said, "Do not commit adultery". But I tell you that anyone who looks at a woman lustfully has already committed adultery with her in his heart. If your right eye causes you to sin, gouge it out and throw it away. It is better for you to lose one part of your body than for your whole body to be thrown into hell. And if your right hand causes you to sin, cut it off and throw it away. It is better for you to lose one part of your body than for your whole body to go hell.

For I tell you the truth, in a world where the outer appearance
of things may seem intriguing and tempting, you may find
yourself basing your actions on what you see on the outside.

In a world where women are seen more as sexual objects
than as humans, it is crucial that you become more aware of
the dangers of going along with the crowd or society.

The world has made it seem unusual for a man to have encounters with
women and not have ulterior motives or sexual desire towards them.

It has become hard for opposite sexes to have interactions without
having the urge or the temptations of adultery. This generation has
been taught that appearances are everything. This generation has
been taught that what makes them beautiful is the clothes they
wear, the make-up they put on, and the places they live in.

For I say to you, do not commit adultery or view every passing
woman or man as a sexual object for you to indulge in. I say this
truth not to change you or turn you into a righteous being, but
because every thought you have of other people comes from you,

every action you do to other people is made up by you, and so every thought and view of other people you have returns to you.

For whatever goes up must come down, whatever goes around must come around. For this sums up the law and life.

So then, if your left eye causes you to see the bad in others, you ought to remove those thoughts. You should rather experience a happy, respectful, and abundant life with one eye than to experience a life of judgment, disrespect, and pain with your whole body still intact.

For the truth is you ought to be careful how you view the world. For one day you will realize you were looking at the mirror all along.

DIVORCE

It is has been said, "Anyone who divorces his wife must give her a certificate of divorce." But I tell you that anyone who divorces his wife except for marital unfaithfulness, causes her to become an adulteress, and anyone who marries the divorced woman commits adultery.

For I tell you the truth, nowadays the pressure of getting married and having a family of your own has ironically led to the increasing number of divorces we see around the world – a life that has already been set up for you, or so you thought.

For the truth is you spend most of your life trying to find another person that will complete your happiness and the person you think completes you. You spend your life trying to find someone and ignore the importance of first finding yourself.

For you may have been told that if you are no longer in love in your marriage, you ought to seek a divorce. But I say to you, before you seek a person you are going to spend the rest of your life with, first seek the person you have been spending the whole of your life with.

For the moment you start looking for someone to love you, you ought to make sure that you love yourself first. You cannot expect your wife or husband to love you while you do not love yourself. You cannot expect your wife or husband to know you while you do not know yourself. You cannot expect your wife or husband to make you happy while you cannot make yourself happy. You cannot expect your wife or husband to treat you like everything while you treat yourself as nothing.

For I say to you, before you walk the path of marriage, make sure that you know the person that is going into the marriage. For the truth is anyone who divorces his or her spouse for anything other than for being unfaithful becomes vulnerable to the path of destruction.

For I say to you, do not go into marriage with ulterior motives or just for the sake of getting married and moving along with society. Nor must you get married because you have been pressured into marriage. For I tell you the truth, you will waste your life and another person's too, which will certainly be a waste. For nothing will help you when you spend your remaining time looking back in regret.

Again I say to you, when it comes to marriage and divorce, do not rush and go into it without your heart being fully there. I tell you the truth, then you will have no reason to divorce your wife or husband.

OATHS

Again you have heard that it was said to the people long ago, "Do not break your oath, but keep the oaths you have made to the Lord." But I tell you, do not swear at all, either by heaven, for it is God's throne, or by the earth, for it is his footstool. And do not swear by your head, for you cannot make even one hair white or black. Simply let your "Yes" be yes and your "No" be no. Anything beyond this comes from the evil one.

The truth is a hard thing to come by these days. For you live in a world where rather than being told the truth, you are more likely to be fed what you would like to hear. This has led more people to make promises they know they cannot keep or to make comments just so to impress others with half-baked truths.

For the truth is when we say things or make promises to others, we not only make promises to them, but also to ourselves. You may have thought for a long time that you were lying to them, but I tell you the truth, you have been lying to yourself all along.

For the truth is every oath and promise you make to other people comes from you. And so every oath and promise you make to others will certainly return to you.

For I tell you the truth, not to change the person you are nor to change the way you behave with other people, but I tell you the truth so you may know that whatever you do and say to other people will be what others do and say to you. For this sums up the law and life.

For I tell you the truth, you must resist the urge and the need to impress other people in an effort to protect or please yourself or someone else. For when you are truthful, it does not mean that you are rude or hateful. Maybe it is better during those times that you simply say nothing. But I tell you the truth, when you do speak up, make sure you say what you want to say and what you really mean.

For I tell you the truth, simply let your "Yes" be a yes and let your "No" be a no. Never let yourself be in a position where you are saying yes to others but in the meantime you are whispering no to yourself.

For the biggest mistake you can ever make is living a life in which you are imprisoned by what other people think of you. For I tell you the truth, they are not bothered by you because they too are busy being worried about what other people are thinking of them.

For I say to you, be true to yourself and with others. Every time you are with a person, be sure it is not just your lips moving for the sake of them moving, but make sure it is your soul truly expressing itself. For I tell you the truth, everything you say and do comes from you. Everything you say and do is made up from you. And so everything you say and do returns to you.

AN EYE FOR AN EYE

You have heard that it was said, "Eye for eye and tooth for tooth." But I tell you, do not resist an evil person. If someone strikes you on the right cheek, turn to him the other also. And if someone wants to sue you and take your tunic, let him have your cloak as well. If someone forces you to go one mile, go with him two miles. Give to the one who asks you, and do not turn away from the one who wants to borrow from you.

For I tell you the truth, often we do things for people because we expect them to do the same for us, only to find ourselves disappointed. For I tell you the truth, in the end it will not be between you and people, but it will be between you and God. For people will often be unreasonable and self-centred. For I say to you, forgive them anyway. For if you are kind, people may accuse you of having ulterior motives. For I say to you, be kind anyway. For if you are honest, people may often take advantage and cheat you. For I say to you, be honest anyway. For if you find happiness, other people may be jealous. For I say to you, be happy anyway. For the good you do today may be forgotten tomorrow. For I say to you, do good anyway. For you may give the world the best you have and it may never be enough. For I say to you, give your best anyway. For I tell you the truth, in the end it is between you and God. It was never between you and them anyway.

For I tell you the truth, the kingdom of God is a place where you give because of the gift of giving, not because of the possibility of receiving; a place where when you love, you love because of the joy you create, not because you expect to be loved, too; a place where when you care, you care because you understand what it feels like, not because you expect the next person to see your deed and be

grateful; a place where when you wish good for someone, you wish
it for their good, not so you can benefit; a place I hope you reach,
not for the sake of others, but for the sake of your own life.

For I tell you the truth, everything comes from everything, and
everything is made up of everything, and so everything returns to
everything. For in life you will encounter difficulties, but what matters
most is how you react. It matters that when you give out good, no matter
what bad there is, you begin to see that what you choose to experience
is what will unfold before your eyes. For the choice is yours to make.
You will be the light that always shines and gives the light it was given
to others because it knows that when it shines and lightens the paths
for others, it doesn't darken its own path and shines over all darkness.

For I tell you the truth, you may choose to be the darkness and the
inferior of light and to let a person pull you low enough to hate
them. For those who resist evil with evil soon find out that they have
created more evil. Those who resist hate with hate soon find out that
they have created more hate. Those who resist violence with violence
soon find out that they have created more violence. Those who resist
war with war soon find out that they have created more war.

For I tell you the truth. Through violence you may murder the liar,
but I tell you the truth, you cannot murder the lie, nor establish
the truth. Through violence you may murder the hater, but I tell
you the truth, you do not murder hate. Through violence you may
murder the criminal, but I tell you the truth, you cannot murder
crime. Through violence you may murder the rapist, but I tell you the
truth, you do not murder rape. Through violence you may murder
the violent, but I tell you the truth, you do not murder violence.

For I tell you the truth, darkness cannot drive out darkness; only
light can do that. Hate cannot drive out hate; only love can do that.
In life you choose to be the light of the world or the darkness.

Again I say to you, do not resist an evil person. If someone
strikes you on the right cheek, turn to him the other also. And

if someone wants to sue you and take your tunic, let him have your cloak as well. If someone forces you to go one mile, go with him two miles. Give to the one who asks you, and do not turn away from the one who wants to borrow from you.

For I tell you the truth, every evil you return with evil comes from you, and every evil you return with evil is made up from you. And so every evil you return with evil returns to you, for in the end it will only be between you and the Creator.

LOVE FOR ENEMIES

You have heard that it was said, "Love your neighbour and hate your enemy." But I tell you, love your enemies, bless those who curse you, do good to those who hate you, and pray for those who persecute you, that you may be sons of your Father in heaven. He causes his sun to rise on the evil and the good, and sends rain on the righteous and the unrighteous. If you love only those who love you, what reward will you get? Are not even the tax collectors doing that? And if you greet only your brothers, what are you doing more than others? Be perfect, therefore, as your heavenly Father is perfect.

For I tell you the truth, till this day you have been living a life
where it is normal to love those who love you, to hate those
who hate you, and to ignore those who do not know you.

For the truth is you have been living your life based on the
principles of having close relationships with your family
members and your friends. Whether you are a child or
an adult, your whole life has been based upon waking up
with your family and going to work with your colleagues.
After that you meet with your close friends, and soon after
that you go back to the loving arms of your family.

For I tell you the truth, many people who are quick to
tell others that they are the righteous sons and daughters
of the Son of man seem to be quite the opposite of
what the Son of man was and what he stood for.

It seems many people have the wrong idea of what it means to be righteous and to be the exact image of the Creator or what it means to enter through the Son of man to get to the kingdom of the Creator.

For I tell you the truth, being righteous does not involve spending the whole week in the pursuit of money and on the last day of the week singing and shouting at the top of your voice. Being righteous does not involve you being accepted as part of a religion or a tradition. Being righteous does not involve you doing nothing.

For I tell you the truth, your beliefs do not make you a good person; your actions do. For I tell you the truth, your place of work does not make you a good person; your actions do. For I tell you the truth, your clothes and money do not make you a good person; your actions do.

For I tell you the truth, the Son of man said you should love your enemies, bless those who curse you, do good to those who hate you, and pray for those who persecute you, so that you may be sons of your Father in heaven. He causes his sun to rise on the evil and the good, and sends rain on the righteous and the unrighteous.

For I tell you the truth, the Son of man did not say those things just so you can be a good and righteous person. He said those things so you would know that every person you give or do not give love to comes from you, and so every person you give or do not give love to returns to you.

For the truth is you seem to think that the Creator separates you, your thoughts, and your feelings from the rest of the world and people around you. This delusion has created a prison for you, restricting you to your own personal desires and your affection towards a few people nearest to you.

For I tell you the truth, if you seek to enter the kingdom of the Creator, let your thoughts towards every person be pure so your life can also be pure. Let your words towards every person be pure so your life can also be pure. And let your actions

towards every person be pure so your life can also be pure.
For I tell you the truth, the love you give those closest to you
has the same measure as the love you deny every stranger.

So then, let your love be like the love the Creator gives.
By this you will not only be like your Creator in heaven,
but you will also have heaven within you.

GIVING TO THE NEEDY

Be careful not to do your acts of righteousness before men, to be seen by them. If you do, you will have no reward from your Father in heaven. So when you give to the needy, do not announce it with trumpets, as the hypocrites do in the synagogues and on the street, to be honoured by men. I tell you the truth, they have received their reward in full. But when you give to the needy, do not let your left hand know what your right hand is doing, so that your giving may be in secret. Then your Father, who sees what is done in secret, will reward you.

For I say to you, be careful that you do not do your acts of good just so other people can see your good deeds and see you as a righteous person. Do not be like the rich men and women who make it known to the world at charity events that they have done good for the less fortunate. Do not be like the people in churches who make it known to the world that they are doing greater good for the less fortunate. Do not be like the politicians who make it known to the world the good that they are doing for people in disadvantaged communities.

For the truth is you may fool some people some of the time, you may fool some people all of the time, you may fool all people some of the time, but I tell you the truth, you cannot fool all people all of the time. For what you do not understand is that whenever you are lying to people, the person you are actually lying to is yourself. But I tell you the truth, the voices in your head are heard not only by you, but by the Creator, too.

For I tell you the truth, whatever intentions you hold in your heart come from you. Whatever intentions you hold in your heart are made up from you. And the truth is whatever intentions you hold in your heart return to you. For whatever you may give comes from you, whatever you may give is made up from you, and so whatever you give returns to you.

Whenever you give to those in need, make sure that you give with no ulterior motives. For the truth is whatever you receive will have no ulterior motives. Whenever you give to those in need, make sure that you give with a pure, open heart. For the truth is whatever you will receive will be abundantly pure. Whenever you give to those in need, make sure that you give, not for the sake of other people. For the truth is whatever you receive will be for your own sake.

For I say to you, give to the one who is in need, open for the one who knocks, never turn away from the one who asks, walk with the one who is in fear, bless the one who persecutes you, and most of all love each and every thing you see in front of you.

PRAYER

And when you pray, do not be like the hypocrites, for they love to pray standing in the synagogues and on the street corners to be seen by men. I tell you the truth, they have received their reward in full. But when you pray, go into your room, close the door, and pray to your Father, who is unseen. Then your Father, who sees what is being done in secret, will reward you. And when you pray, do not be like the pagans, for they think they will be heard because of their many words. Do not be like them, for your Father knows what you need before you ask him.

This then is how you should pray.

"Our Father in heaven, hallowed be your name. Your kingdom come, your will be done, on earth as it is in heaven. Give us today our daily bread; forgive us our debts, as we also have forgiven our debtors. And lead us not into temptation, but deliver us from evil, for yours is the kingdom and the power and the glory forever. Amen."

For if you forgive men when they sin against you, your heavenly Father will also forgive you. But if you do not forgive men their sins, your father will not forgive your sins."

For I tell you the truth, prayer is your soul is talking to the Creator.
So then when you pray, do not be like the people in churches and
in places of worship who think their prayers will be answered
because of the loudness they make and the many words they
proclaim, some of them shouting in tongues. And do not be like
those who make it known to other people that they are praying.

For I tell you the truth, when you pray, there is no need for you
to even close your eyes and utter many words, for the truth is just
as you already know what you want and desire in your heart, the
Creator that is within you already knows what you really need.

For the truth is many people seem to think that the Creator is far away
from them. They seem to think that the Creator is a man living in the
sky. They seem to think that the Creator is watching them from afar.
They seem to think that the Creator listens only when they get down
on their knees. But I tell you the truth, the Creator is within you.

For I say to you, when you pray, do not be like the hypocrites you
see at gatherings who shout out loud to be heard by others, because
I tell you the truth, the Creator is within you. When you pray, do
not be like the hypocrites you see at gatherings who utter many
words and speak in tongues, because I tell you the truth, the Creator
is within you. When you pray, do not be like the hypocrites you
see at gatherings who stand in front of crowds to be seen by other
men, because I tell you the truth, the Creator is within you.

For the truth is whatever you have in your heart is a prayer
that you continue praying even without noticing. Whatever
you have in your mind is a prayer that you continue praying
even without noticing. Whatever you have in your words is a
prayer that you continue praying even without noticing.

TREASURES IN HEAVEN

Do not store up for yourselves treasures on earth, where moth and rust destroy, and where thieves break in and steal. But store up for yourselves treasures in heaven, where moth and rust do not destroy, and where thieves do not break in and steal. For where your treasure is, there your heart will be also.

The eye is the lamp of the body. If your eyes are good, your whole body will be full of light. But if your eyes are bad, your whole body will be full of darkness. If then the light within you is darkness, how great is that darkness!

No one can serve two masters. Either he will hate the one and love the other, or he will be devoted to the one and despise the other. You cannot serve both God and money.

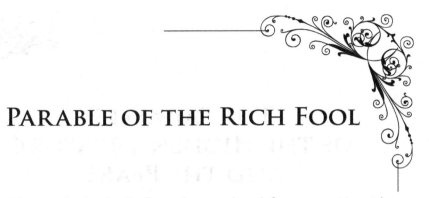

PARABLE OF THE RICH FOOL

A rich man had a fertile farm that produced fine crops. He said to himself, "What should I do? I do not have room for all my crops." Then he said, "I know! I'll tear down my barns and build bigger ones. Then I'll have room enough to store all my wheat and other goods. And I will sit back and say to myself, 'My friend, you have enough stored away for years to come. Now take it easy! Eat, drink, and be merry!'"

But God said to him, "You fool! You will die this very night. Then who will get everything you have worked for?" Yes, a person is a fool to store up earthy wealth but not have a rich relationship with God.

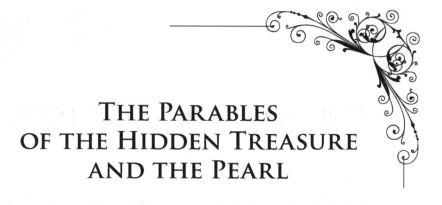

THE PARABLES
OF THE HIDDEN TREASURE
AND THE PEARL

The kingdom of heaven is like treasure hidden in a field. When a man found it, he hid it again, and then in his joy went and sold all he had and bought that field.

Again, the kingdom of heaven is like a merchant looking for fine pearls. When he found one of great value, he went away and sold everything he had and bought it.

For I tell you the truth, you may have been led to think that the true treasures in life are the diamonds, the gold, the money, and the material things that seem to shine in your eyes. But I tell you the truth, true treasures last forever. For the truth is just as the sun rises and then sets again, so will the treasures of the earth shine in a moment but turn to dust the next moment. Just as the stars shine brightly at night and disappear during the day, so can thieves smile at your earthly treasure during the day, then break in and steal it late at night.

For say to you, do not store up for yourselves treasure of the world where one day they are here and the next they are nowhere to be found. Do not store up for yourselves treasures of the world where one day they shine brightly in eyes and the next they are dirty dust in the ground. Do not store up for yourselves treasures of the world where one day they are safely stored in your safe and the next they are in the safe hands of thieves and robbers.

For the truth is you spend your life in the pursuit of the treasures of the earth. You have spent years upon years building buildings, and in the end they have built you. Your whole life is based on getting up in the morning, getting dressed in clothes that you buy for work, driving through traffic in a car that you are still paying for, and getting to a job that you need so you can pay for the clothes, cars, and house that you leave empty all day in order to afford to live in it.

For I tell you the truth, deep within you dwells a desire for the treasures of heaven like happiness, like peace, like freedom, like abundance and prosperity. For the sad truth is that you seek first the kingdom of earth and all its shiny treasures and expect that the things of the kingdom of the Creator will fall at your feet. All your days from Monday right through to Sunday are dedicated to the pursuit of money and worldly treasures. But I tell you the truth, you cannot serve both the Creator and money.

For I tell you the truth, whatever you hold dear in your heart will be the destiny that will unfold right before your eyes. For if your heart is filled with the desire of money, your whole life will be solely focused on money. And just as it comes this moment and vanishes the next, you place your heart, mind, and soul on what will soon be dust and ashes.

For you have neglected your purpose given to you by the Creator to base the life you live on the biggest treasure from the kingdom of heaven, which no thief nor robber can take away and steal, which no rust nor moth can destroy, which can stand the test of time. For the truth is the light inside you has been darkened by the sight of shiny objects in front of you.

For I say to you, store up for yourselves treasures from the kingdom of heaven. For when you store up love, no number of moths or amount of rust can destroy it. When you store up imagination, no amount of thieves or robbers can steal it. When you store up peace, no amount of moths or rust can destroy it. When you store up righteousness, no amount of thieves or robbers can destroy it. When you store up hope, no amount of moths or rust can destroy it.

For I tell you the truth, you cannot store up for yourself money
and expect to find happiness. You cannot store up for yourself gold
and expect to find peace. You cannot store up for yourself houses
and expect to find security and protection. You cannot store up for
yourself cars and clothes and expect to find love. You cannot store up
for yourself diamonds and gadgets and expect to find imagination.

For the truth is you seek all these treasures in order to find
the true treasure of heaven. But I tell you the truth, you
cannot seek earthly treasures and expect to find the Creator.
For I tell you the truth, that is why you cannot serve two
masters, as you will be loyal to one and neglect the other.

For whatever you hold close to your heart will be what you become.
Whatever treasure you hold dear to you will be what you serve. For
again I say to you, the money and earthly treasures go to dust and other
people, your body goes to the earth, and your soul goes to the Creator.

DO NOT WORRY

Therefore I tell you, do not worry about your life, what you will eat or drink or about your body, what you will wear. Is not life more important than food and the body more important than clothes?

Look at the birds of the air; they do not sow or reap or store away in barns and yet your heavenly Father feeds them. Are you not much more valuable than they? Who of you by worrying can add a single hour to his life?

And why do you worry about clothes? See how the lilies of the field grow, they do not labour or spin. Yet I tell you that not even Solomon in all his splendour was dressed like one these. If that is how God clothes the grass of the field, which is here today and tomorrow thrown into the fire, will he not much more clothe you, O you of little faith? So do not worry, saying, "What shall we eat?" or, "What shall we drink?" or, "What shall we wear?" For the pagans run after all these things, and your heavenly Father knows that you need them. But seek first his kingdom and his righteousness and all these things will be given to you as well. Therefore do not worry about tomorrow, for tomorrow will worry about itself. Each day has enough trouble of its own.

So don't be afraid, little flock, for it gives your father great happiness to give you the kingdom. Sell your possessions and give to those in need. For this will store up treasure for you in heaven! And the purses of heaven never get old or develop holes. Your treasure will be safe. No thief can steal it and no moth can destroy it. Wherever your treasure is, there the desires of your heart will also be.

For I tell you the truth, you spend your days in the pursuit of money because of the worries you have. You spend your days in a constant battle over what will you eat when you are hungry. You spend your days in a constant battle over what will you wear when you are cold. You spend your days in a constant battle over where you will sleep when the night arrives. But I tell you the truth, you will not gain anything by spending your days full of worry.

For the truth is when you start worrying about what you will eat, what you will drink, what you will wear, or where you will sleep, you begin to seek the treasures of the world, and soon enough you will be filled with more worries than you could ever handle.

For if you seek first the kingdom of the Creator and its righteousness, all these other things will be given to you. And I tell you the truth, no amount of worry can ever enter your mind.

For I tell you the truth, instead of worrying about what you will eat, embrace the happiness around you and I tell you the truth, not only will your stomach be filled, but your life will be overflowing with the things that make you happy. Instead of worrying about what you will wear, embrace the peace around you and I tell you the truth, not only will your body be kept warm, clothed, and safe, but your life will be overflowing with the things that bring you peace. Instead of worrying about where you will sleep, embrace the love around you and I tell you the truth, not only will you have the protection and security, but your life and soul will have a home in eternity.

So then I say to you again, just as the flowers of the desert that at one moment seem to have no chance of growing, I tell you the truth, whenever they need rain, whenever they need warmth, whenever they need air, it is provided for them. For if you seek first the kingdom of the Creator, everything you need will be provided for you.

For I tell you the truth, little one, the Creator wants you to have all the things you can ever imagine. But the truth is you first have to seek the Creator, and you shall find all that you seek and deserve. Seek first the peace within you, and you will find peace in the world. Seek first the love within you, and you will find love in the world. Seek first the joy within you, and you will find joy in the world. Seek first all the things money and worry cannot buy and all shall be added to you.

For the truth is if you believe in the Creator, you should be ashamed of even worrying about anything in life. But I tell you the truth, do not worry about the things that are here today and gone tomorrow. The Creator knows you need some of them. Focus on the things that are with you forever, for in the end it will not be between you and the world, but it will be between you and the Creator.

Judging Others

Do not judge, or you too will be judged. For in the same way as you have judged others, you will be judged, and in the same measure you use, it will be measured to you.

Why do you look at the speck of sawdust in your brother's eye and pay no attention to the plank in your own eye? How can you say to your brother, "Let me take the speck out of your eye," when all the time there is a plank in your own eye? You hypocrite, first take out the plank out of your own eye, and then you will see clearly to remove the speck from your brother's eye.

Do not give to dogs what is sacred, do not throw your pearls to pigs. If you do, they may trample them under their feet and then turn and tear you to pieces.

For I say to you, never be quick to point fingers and judge people.
For at times we are so quick to point fingers at people that we
forget there are always three fingers pointing back at us.

We are quick to point out the wrong in other people and so effortlessly
forget our own faults. We are quick to point out the limits of others
but forget that we are not even near perfect. For I tell you the truth,
when you judge others, you judge only yourself, for every judgment
you give, the same measure of judgment will be given to you.

For I tell you the truth, every judgment you make comes
from you, every judgment you make is made up from you,
and so every judgment you make returns to you.

For the truth is whatever you say about others says a lot about you. Whatever you think about others creates what people think of you. Whatever you do to others determines how people will treat you.

For I say to you, keep you thoughts about other people positive because your thoughts will become your words. Keep your words about other people positive because your words will become your actions. Keep your actions towards other people positive because your actions will become your behaviour. keep your behaviour towards other people positive because your behaviour will become your habits. Keep your habits towards other people positive because your habits will become your values. Keep your values towards others people positive because your values will become your destiny. And I tell you the truth, your destiny is to love others as you would like to be loved. For the truth is when you judge people, you have no time to love them.

Give kindness everywhere you go, give love everywhere you go, give hope everywhere you go, give peace everywhere you go, give joy everywhere you go. For then you will be perfect. Let the light within shine over the darkness you see in other people. Then you will be able to show people the way.

For I tell you this truth not to change who you are or to make you into a good person. But I tell you the truth so that you may understand that every judgment you make comes from you, every judgment you make is made up from you, and so every judgment you make returns to you.

So then I say to you again, seek for the good in people instead of judging the bad in them. Seek for the love in people instead of judging the hate in them. Seek for the joy in other people instead of judging the negativity in them. Seek for the beauty in other people instead of judging the ugly in them.

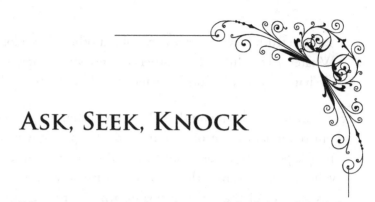

ASK, SEEK, KNOCK

Ask and it will be given to you, seek and you will find, knock and the door will be opened to you. For everyone who asks receives, he who seeks finds and to him who knocks, the door will be opened.

Which of you, if his Son asks for bread, will give him a stone? Or if he asks for a fish, will give him a snake? If you, then, though you are evil, know how to give good gifts to your children, how much more will your Father in heaven give good gifts to those who ask him! So in everything, do to others what you would have them do to you, for this sums up the Law and the Prophets.

Suppose you went to a friend's house at midnight, wanting to borrow three loaves of bread. You say to him, "A friend of mine just arrived for a visit, and I have nothing for him to eat." And suppose he calls out from his bedroom, "Don't bother me. The door is locked for the night and my family and I are in bed. I cannot help you." But I tell you this – though he will not do it for friendship's sake, if you keep knocking long enough, he will get up and give whatever you need because of your shameless persistence. And so I tell you, keep on asking, and you will receive what you ask for, keep on seeking and you will find what you seek, keep on knocking and the door will be opened for you. For the one who asks shall receive, the one who seeks shall find, and the one who knocks the door shall be opened for them.

You are the child of the Creator, for if you ask, you will be given; for if you knock, the door will be opened for you; for if you search, you will find. For whoever asks from the heart will be given in life. For whoever knocks at the door of the kingdom of heaven, the door of happiness, peace and love will be opened. For whoever searches for the truth, love, and abundance will find an abundance of love, peace, and happiness.

You are the light of the world. What you ask for with your mind and heart you receive in life. For if you ask for good, love, abundance, and peace, you will receive with the same measure the good, love, abundance, and peace you have given.

You are the writer of the story of your life. For if you knock on the door with love, peace, and happiness, the door of an abundance of love, peace, and happiness opens up.

You are the master of your destiny. For if you search for love, peace, and happiness, you will find an abundance of love, peace, and happiness.

For God so loved his children that He gave them the power to choose anything they want, the power to choose any path they wish to go, the power to choose what they want to create in their lives, the power to create the world they want from within.

But do not ask with your mind and heart for the bad, the jealousy, the hate, or the sadness. For I tell the truth, you will be given the bad, the jealousy, the hate, and the sadness. Do not knock at the door with hate, sadness, jealousy, and anger. For I tell you the truth, the door of hate, sadness, jealousy, and anger will be opened for you. Do not search for hate, anger, sadness, and jealousy, for I tell you the truth, you will find hate, anger, sadness, and jealousy all around you.

For none of you would give your son a rock when he asks for bread nor a snake when he asks for a fish. As it is with the parent and son, so it is with your Father in heaven and you.

For you must treat others the way you want be treated. In everything do to others what you would like done to you by others, for this is the foundation of the Law.

For everything you seek comes from everything,
everything you seek is made up from everything, and
so everything you seek returns to everything.

For I tell you the truth, whatever your heart and soul may desire will
be given to you if you keep on seeking, knocking, and asking. For the
truth is you are the creation that creates; you are the light that ignites
others. Let your heart be free, and it will receive the fulfilment it desires.

For I tell you the truth, you are what you think, not what
you think you are. Think about it – now think about it.

THE NARROW
AND WIDE GATES

Enter through the narrow gate. For wide is the gate and broad is the road that leads to destruction, and many enter through it. But small is the gate and narrow the road that leads to life, and only a few find it.

For I say to you, enter the kingdom of the Creator through the narrow gate, and do not attempt to enter the kingdom of the Creator through the wide gate. For the truth is only a few find the way to the narrow gate and walk paths of life in the way of righteousness, the way of love, the way of peace, the way of hope, the way of joy, the way of prosperity, the way of unity, and the way of the Son of man.

For the truth is many have found the wide gate that has led them to the path of the kingdom of earth, for many have found the wide gate and thought that it leads to life. For I tell you the truth, the gate to the kingdom is not in the path of religions. The gate to the kingdom is not in the path of money. The gate to the kingdom is not in the path of worshipping. The gate to the kingdom is not in the path of a book. The gate to the kingdom is not in the path of division.

For I say to you, do not attempt to enter the kingdom of the Creator by being part of a religion, for the truth is the Creator has no religion. Do not attempt to enter the kingdom of the Creator by going to church, for the truth is going to church will never make you a good person – your behaviour does.

For the truth is the narrow gate is the path in which you will find the way to the kingdom of the Creator. For I tell you the truth, the way to the kingdom is through love; the way to the kingdom is through peace; the way to the kingdom is through righteousness; the way to the kingdom is through faith; the way to the kingdom is through unity.

So again I say to you, enter through the narrow gate, for the wide gate is filled with paths to destruction. Let your heart seek first the kingdom of the Creator and all the righteousness that comes with it, and you will find the narrow gate.

THE SHEEP AND THE GOATS

When the Son of man comes in his glory, and all the angels with him, he will sit on his throne in heavenly glory. All the nations will be gathered before him, and he will separate the people one from another as a shepherd separates the sheep from the goats, the sheep on his right and the goats on his left.

Then the king will say to those on his right, "Come you who are blessed by my Father, take your inheritance, the kingdom prepared for you since the creation of the world. For I was hungry and you gave me something to eat; I was thirsty and you gave me something to drink; I was a stranger and you invited me in; I needed clothes and you clothed me; I was sick and you looked after me; I was in prison and you came to visit me."

Then the righteous will answer him, "Lord, when did we see you hungry and feed you, or thirsty and give you something to drink? When did we see you a stranger and invite you in, or needing clothes and clothe you? When did we see you sick or in prison and go to visit you?"

The king will reply, "I tell you the truth, what ever you did for one of the least of these brothers of mine, you did for me."

Then he will say to those on his left, "Depart from me, you who are cursed, into the eternal fire prepared for the Devil and his angels. For I was hungry and you gave me nothing to eat; I was thirsty and you gave me nothing to drink; I was a stranger and you did not invite me in; I needed clothes and you did not clothe me; I was sick and in prison and you did not look after me."

They also will answer, "Lord, when did we see you hungry or thirsty or needing clothes or sick or in prison, and did not help you?"

He will reply, "I tell you the truth, whatever you did not do for one of the least of these, you did not do for me." Then they will go away to eternal punishment, but the righteous to eternal life.

For I tell you the truth, when the Son of man returns to gather people as a shepherd gathers his flocks when it is time to return home, it will not be like what people are told, where the Son of man will gather people who call themselves Christians and leave those who did not become part of a religion or proclaim their undying love for him.

For the truth is I have been saying to you that if you seek first the kingdom of the Creator, you will find the treasures of heaven beneath your feet. If you seek first to enter through the narrow gate and walk the path of peace, walk the path of love, walk the path of giving, walk the path of righteousness, walk the path of hope, walk the path that the Son of man walked, you will most certainly find the kingdom of the Creator.

For just as the shepherd separates the sheep from the goats, the people will also be separated. The righteous ones will be on his right and the unrighteous ones will be on his left.

For I tell you the truth, I have been saying to you, if you spend your days in the pursuit of money and the success of this world, your life revolves around making more money so you may live freely in this world. You love only those closest to you and those who may offer you something in return. You believe that the Son of man has paid for the sins you continue to commit. But I tell you the truth, at the end your journey, what will matter will be the very thing you've had all along.

For at the end of our journey, those that walked the path of righteousness will be called and be told, "Come you who are blessed by my Father, take your inheritance, the kingdom prepared for you since the creation of the world. For I was hungry and you gave me something to eat; I was thirsty and you

gave me something to drink; I was a stranger and you invited
me in; I needed clothes and you clothed me; I was sick and you
looked after me; I was in prison and you came to visit me."

For I tell you the truth, these are the people who walked the path by
the way of love, by the way of peace, by the way of unity, by the way
of hope, by the way of giving. For the truth is these are the people who
loved and treated each person the way they would have liked to be loved
and treated. For I tell you the truth, these are the people who lived their
lives just like the Son of man. They gave their time and lives to others. In
the world they were the last, but in the time to come they will be first.

For many will wonder when the righteous people crossed paths with
the Son of man. They will wonder, "Lord, when did we see you hungry
and feed you or thirsty and give you something to drink? When did
we see you a stranger and invite you in or needing clothes and clothe
you? When did we see you sick or in prison and go to visit you?"
But I tell you the truth, the Son of man will reply, "Whatever you
did for one of the least of these brothers of mine, you did for me."

For I tell you the truth, the Son of man will then turn to those on
his left and say to them, "Depart from me, you who are cursed,
into the eternal fire prepared for the Devil and his angels. For I
was hungry and you gave me nothing to eat. I was thirsty and
you gave me nothing to drink. I was a stranger and you did
not invite me in. I needed clothes and you did not clothe me.
I was sick and in prison and you did not look after me."

For I tell you the truth, those who lived their lives in the pursuit
of money and worldly things and who gave their love only to
those closest to them will be left astonished and will wonder
and ask, "Lord, when did we see you hungry or thirsty or
needing clothes or sick or in prison, and did not help you?"

He will reply, "I tell you the truth, whatever you did not do for
one of the least of these, you did not do for me." Then they will go
away to eternal punishment, but the righteous to eternal life.

For I tell you the truth, every person you meet is the Son of man in disguise. Take every opportunity given you to spread more love than hate, to spread more peace than fighting, to spread more hope than discouragement, to spread more joy than tears. For the truth is every way you treat a person comes from you; every way you treat a person is made up from you; and so every way you treat a person returns to you.

For the truth is no amount of visits to the church can ever help a person that needs to be helped. No amount of worship songs you sing can ever feed a person that needs to be fed. No amount of pages you read from a book can clothe a person that needs to be clothed. For I tell you the truth, your beliefs do not make you a better person – your behaviour does.

For I say to you, enter through the narrow gate to the kingdom of the Creator. Let the love inside you be the light in which you enlighten others.

THE PARABLE
OF THE WEDDING BANQUET

The kingdom of heaven is like a king who prepared a wedding banquet for his Son. He sent his servants to those who had been invited to the banquet to tell them to come, but they refused to come. Then he sent some more servants and said, "Tell those who have been invited that I have prepared my dinner, my oxen and fattened cattle have been slaughtered, and everything is ready. Come to the wedding banquet."

But they paid no attention and went off – one to his field, another to his business, the rest seized his servants, ill-treated them, and killed them. The king was enraged. He sent his army and destroyed those murderers and burned their city.

Then he said to his servants, "The wedding banquet is ready, but those I invited did not deserve to come. Go to the street corners and invite to the banquet anyone you find." So the servants went out into the streets and gathered all the people they could find, both good and bad, and the wedding hall was filled with guests.

But when the king came in to see the guests, he noticed a man there who was not wearing wedding clothes. "Friend," he asked, "how did you get in here without wedding clothes?" The man was speechless.

Then the king told the attendants, "Tie him hand and foot, and throw him outside, into the darkness, where there will be weeping and gnashing of teeth."

For many are invited, but few are chosen.

For I tell you the truth, the kingdom of the Creator was prepared for all to come and be in His glory. For just like the wedding banquet, many people were invited. Others heard the call and rose to the occasion. Others heard the call and ignored the calling. Others heard the call and rejected the calling. And others heard the call and just continued living their normal lives.

For I tell you the truth, many people have ignored the call to live life according to the will of our Creator. For the truth is many righteous men and women have risen up and made the call for us to live life with love for ourselves and others as the foundation of our lives.

For I tell you the truth, the Son of man graced this earth and showed us the way to live, but still we ignored the call. Mother Teresa graced this earth and showed us the way to live, but still we ignored the call. Martin Luther King graced this earth and showed us the way to live, but still we ignored the call. Helen Keller graced this earth and showed us the way to live, but still we ignored the call. Mahatma Gandhi graced this earth and showed us the way to live, but still we ignored the call. Albert Einstein graced this earth and showed us the way to live, but still we ignored the call. Finally, Nelson Mandela graced this earth and showed us the way to live, but still we ignored the call.

For the truth is the call to come together and rise as one has been ignored by the masses. But I tell you the truth, many were called and few were chosen. For you may see the days and weeks passing and see that there is no change. But I tell you the truth, as soon you start to look back, you will start to wonder how everything has changed.

For when the times comes, there will be no more calls and trumpets to make people aware of what is to come. The doors to the banquet of heaven will be shut forever. The jobs and houses that once seemed to be everything will be no more than regretful memory.

For I tell you the truth, if you are still able to lay your eyes on these words that are echoing in your mind at this moment, the time to hear the call for the banquet to the kingdom is now. Let the light within you spark once again, for the truth is you were not only called, but I tell you the truth, you were chosen.

THE PARABLE OF THE WEEDS

The kingdom of heaven is like a man who sowed good seed in his field. But while everyone was sleeping, his enemy came and sowed weeds among the wheat and went away. When the wheat sprouted and formed ears, then the weeds also appeared.

The owner's servants came to him and said, "Sir, didn't you sow good seed in your field? Where then did the weeds come from?" "An enemy did this," he replied. The servants asked him, "Do you want us to go and pull them up?" "No," he answered, "because while you are pulling the weeds, you may uproot the wheat with them. Let both grow together until the harvest. At that time I will tell the harvesters, 'First collect the weeds and tie them in bundles to be burned. Then gather the wheat and bring it into my barn.'"

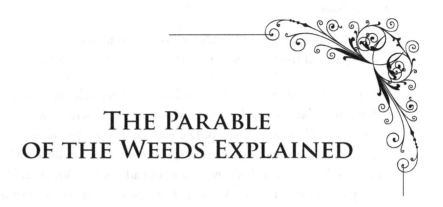

THE PARABLE
OF THE WEEDS EXPLAINED

The one who sowed the good seed is the Son of man. The field is the world, and the good seed stands for the sons of the kingdom. The weeds are the sons of the evil one, and the enemy who sows them is the Devil. The harvest is the end of the age, and the harvesters are angels.

As the weeds are pulled up and burned in the fire, so it will be at the end of age. The Son of man will send out his angels, and they will weed out of his kingdom everything that causes sin and all who do evil. They will throw them into the fiery furnace, where there will be weeping and gnashing of teeth. Then the righteous will shine like the sun in the kingdom of their Father. He who has ears, let him hear.

For I tell you the truth, every seed that is planted into the earth
soon grows into a tree. That tree will either serve its purpose for
good or it will serve its purpose for bad. But I tell you the truth,
there comes a time to cut down every tree that was once a seed.
Others were useful for fruits and great shade. Others were wasteful
as leafless dry trees. For the truth is the fruitful trees that were once
seeds will be used to plant more seeds and increase in abundance.
The dry trees that never lived their purpose will be cut down
and burnt to increase the fire in the kingdom of destruction.

For the truth is just as in the beginning of the season good seeds were
planted alone, as time went on and they spent their days in the field,
bad seeds started to grow as well. The good seeds were left to grow
together with the bad seeds. But I tell you the truth, when the time

to harvest comes, the good seeds that turned out to be good trees will be separated from the bad seeds that turned out to be bad trees.

For I tell you the truth, we were born children who knew only happiness. Are we to die adults who know only stress? We were born children who knew only curiosity. Are we to die adults who know only what they are told. We were born children who knew only love for others. Are we to die adults who know to love only those closest to us? We were born children who knew only imagination. Are we to die adults who know only what we see? We were born children who knew only the kingdom of the Creator. Are we to die adults who know only the kingdom of earth?

For I tell you the truth, you were born a good seed, a seed that was planted on this earth to thrive in the light. For the truth is either you will let the weeds that grow beside you change the person you were meant to be or you will rise above the weeds and let your light shine upon others.

For the truth is in the beginning we were all good seeds. But I tell you the truth, it is your choice if you turn out to be a tree choked out by weeds that is good only for the fire rather than a fruitful tree that creates an abundance that will be enjoyed for eternity.

THE PARABLE OF THE NET

Once again the kingdom of heaven is like a net that was let down into the lake and caught all kinds of fish. When it was full, the fishermen pulled it up on the shore. Then they sat down and collected the good fish in the baskets but threw the bad away. This is how it will be at the end of the age. The angels will come and separate the wicked from the righteous and throw them into the fiery furnace where there will be weeping and gnashing of teeth.

For I tell you the truth, just as there were good seeds and bad seeds, so too in the end it will be like a great net that is thrown into the ocean to catch all kinds of fish. For the truth is whether in the ocean of life you were a shark or you were a sardine or you were a dolphin or you were a crab, I tell you the truth, when the net of the Creator falls upon you, there will be no escape.

For in the end, both men and women, both the young and the old, both the wise and the ignorant, both the rich and the poor, both the healthy and the sick, both the good and the bad will be separated like fish caught in a net, each one according to the deeds done while in the ocean of life.

For I say to you, do not fool yourself into thinking that when the net of life comes down on us, we will be separated according to what religion each one has chosen or we will be separated according to what one has confessed while in the ocean of life.

For the truth is at this moment you have the choice to walk in the light of love or to walk in the darkness of selfish destructiveness. For I tell you the truth, you have brains in your head; you have feet in your shoes. For the truth is you can steer yourself in any direction you choose.

For I tell you the truth, when the net of life comes down on us all, we all will have had enough time to choose where we stand, to be put aside as good fish or to be put aside as bad fish and thrown away.

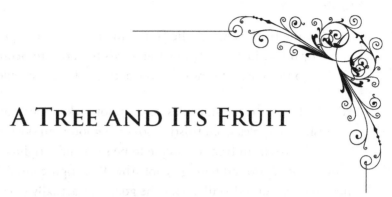

A Tree and Its Fruit

Watch out for false prophets. They come to you in sheep's clothing, but inwardly they are ferocious wolves. By their fruit you will recognize them. Do people pick grapes from thorn bushes or figs from thistles? Likewise every good tree bears good fruit, but a bad tree bears bad fruit. A good tree cannot bear bad fruit and a bad tree cannot bear good fruit. Every tree that does not bear good fruit is cut down and thrown into the fire. Thus by their fruit you will recognize them.

Not everyone who says to me, "Lord, Lord," will enter the kingdom of heaven, but only he who does the will of my Father who is in heaven. Many will say to me on that day, "Lord, Lord, did we not prophesy in your name, and in your name drive out demons and perform many miracles?" Then I will tell them plainly, "I never knew you. Away from me you evildoers!"

For I say to you, be careful of the people who come to you
looking like God-sent angels. Be careful of people who
clean the outside and neglect cleaning the inside, people
who clean the garden, outside walls, and yard just so others
can see their cleanliness, neglecting the dirty kitchen,
messy bedroom, and filthy lounge they alone dwell in.

For you will continue to hear and see many people who
come to the masses and claim that they are prophets who
are sent by the Creator. But I tell you the truth, by their
actions you will recognize them. Just as a tree is recognized
by its fruits, you will see them by their actions.

For the truth is just as the Son of man was first recognized
by his actions and not by the words he spoke to people,
you too must be aware of the actions of these people.

For I tell you the truth, just as you cannot pick grapes from thorn
bushes or apples from thistles, so too a good man does not do
his good deeds in front of people to be seen and a righteous man
does not go around telling people that he is righteous. A loving
person does not only talk about the good but actually does good. A
powerful person does not go around telling people he is powerful;
you see his power for yourself. A generous person does not go
around telling people he is generous; you just see his generosity.

For the truth is many people will continue to fool the masses by
just cleaning the outside and putting titles to their names. But I
tell you the truth, by their actions you will recognize them.

Many will be misled by the false prophets who fool people into
thinking that everyone who calls the Son of man "Lord, Lord"
will enter the kingdom of the Creator, but I tell you the truth, not
everyone who calls the Son of man "Lord" will enter the kingdom
of the Creator, but only those who do the will of the Creator to
love each and every person as they would like to be loved.

For I tell you the truth, when the end arrives, many will be proclaiming
to the Son of man, "Lord, did we not prophesy in your name and
in your name drive out demons and perform miracles? Did we
not worship your name and sing songs to declare our love for you?
Did we not spend our Sundays calling out your name and giving
you praise?" For I tell you the truth, the Son of man will turn to
them and say, "Away from me, you evildoers. I never knew you."

For I say to you, do not be fooled by those who call themselves
prophets but fail to see the truth. It is your behaviour that will
make you do the will of the Creator, not your beliefs. It is your
actions and your deeds that will determine what fruit you will
bear in life, not your words or promises. For the truth is the Son of

man did not grace this earth to die for your sins and wrongdoing. He graced this earth to show you the way to the light.

For the truth is it is up to you now how you will live your life. But I tell you the truth, in the end, only you will be liable for the deeds you did and did not do while here on earth. When the day arrives for you to meet the Creator, not even the Son of man can help you.

THE WISE AND FOOLISH BUILDERS

Therefore everyone who hears these words of mine and puts them into practice is like a wise man who built his house on the rock. The rain came down, the streams rose, and the wind blew and beat against that house, yet it did not fall because it had its foundation on the rock. But everyone who hears these words of mine and does not put them into practice is like a foolish man who built his house on sand. The rain came down, the streams rose, and the winds blew and beat against that house, and it fell with a great crash.

> For I say to you, if you have ears, do not just hear but listen; if you have eyes, do not see but perceive; if you have a mind, do not just memorize but understand.

For the truth is if you understand these words I say to you and put them into practice, I tell you the truth, you will place a solid foundation for your soul like the pig who built his house on rock with bricks and stones. The wolves came and huffed and puffed and huffed and puffed. The rain came down, the streams rose, and the wind blew, but still that house did not fall because it had its foundation on a rock.

For I say to you, place the foundation of your soul on the rock which is love. Place the foundation of your soul on the rock which is peace. Place the foundation of your soul on the rock which is unity. Place the foundation of your soul on the rock which is righteousness. Place the foundation of your soul on the rock which is prosperity. Place the foundation of your soul on the rock which is faith. Place the foundation of your soul on the rock which is generosity. Place the foundation of your soul on the rock which is happiness.

For no matter how much rain comes, no matter how many streams rise, no matter how much the wind blows, no matter how many thieves try to break in, no matter how many moths come, no matter how much rust there is, your house will not fall.

For I tell you the truth, the money and possessions go to other people, the body goes to the earth, the soul goes to the Creator.

For the truth is if you ignore these words I say to you and continue living according to the world, you will have placed no foundation for your soul. Like the pig who built his house on sand with straw and mud, the wolves came and huffed and puffed and huffed and puffed, the rain came down, the streams rose, the wind blew and beat against that house, and it fell with a great crash.

For I say to you, do not place your soul on the sand which is money that is here today and gone tomorrow. Do not place your soul on the sand which is buildings. Do not place your soul on the sand which is hate that only multiplies the very hate it's trying to diminish. Do not place your soul on the sand which is selfishness that eventually eats the hand that feeds it.

For the truth is as the rain comes, as the streams rise, as the wind blows, as thieves break in, as moths gather, as rust dominates, your house will fall.

For I tell you the truth, the money and possessions go to other people, the body goes to the earth, the soul goes to the Creator.

For if you have ears, do not just hear but listen. If you have eyes, do not just look but see. If you have a mind, do not just perceive but understand.

THE GREATEST IN
THE KINGDOM OF HEAVEN

I tell you the truth, unless you change and become like little children, you will never enter the kingdom of heaven. Therefore, whoever humbles himself like this child is the greatest in the kingdom of heaven.

And whoever welcomes a little child like this in my name welcomes me. But if anyone causes one of these little ones who believe in me to sin, it would be better for him to have a large millstone hung around his neck and to be drowned in the depths of the sea. Woe to the world because of the things that cause people to sin! Such things must come, but woe to the man through whom they come! If your hand or foot causes you to sin, cut it off and throw it away. It is better for you to enter life maimed or crippled than to have two hands or two feet and be thrown into the eternal fire. And if your eye causes you to sin, gouge it out and throw it away. It is better for you to enter life with one eye than to have two eyes and be thrown into the fire of hell.

For I tell you the truth, you were born a child who only knew and wanted love. You were born a child who only knew and wanted hope. You were born a child who only knew and wanted joy. You were born a child who only knew and wanted prosperity. You were born a child who only knew and wanted unity. You born a child that only knew and wanted imagination. You were born a child who only knew and wanted abundance. You were born a child who only knew and wanted faith.

For I say to you, do not let the world turn you into an adult who knows only the pursuit of money. Do not let the world turn you into an adult who knows only greed. Do not let the world turn you into an adult who knows only stress. Do not let the world turn you into an adult who knows only division. Do not let the world turn you into an adult who knows only material things. Do not let the world turn you into an adult who knows only hate. Do not let the world turn you into an adult who knows only scarcity. Do not let the world turn you into an adult who knows only negativity.

For the truth is if you change and become like children, you will enter the kingdom of heaven through the narrow gate of love; you will enter the kingdom of heaven through the narrow gate of unity; you will enter the kingdom of heaven through the narrow gate of joy; you will enter the kingdom of heaven through the narrow gate of righteousness; you will enter the kingdom of heaven through the narrow gate of faith; you will enter the kingdom of heaven through narrow gate of the Son of man.

For I tell you the truth, the world continues to educate the mind without educating the heart. The world continues to teach you the pursuit of money. The world continues to teach you selfishness. The world continues to teach you war. The world continues to teach you scarcity. The world continues to teach you hate. The world continues to teach you negativity. And the world calls it education.

For I say to you, do not let the world limit your love and change the inner child in you. For the truth is only those who change and become like little children will enter the kingdom of heaven. For I tell you the truth, if you can still read these words of mine, you have not lost all your innocence.

For I tell you the truth, those that continue to teach young ones the way of hate, those that continue to teach young ones the way of money, those that continue to teach young ones the way of scarcity, those that continue to teach young ones the way of material things, those that continue to teach young ones the way of the world, and those who neglect to teach them the way of the heart, I tell you the truth, they will soon perish.

For the truth is you were certainly not brought into this life to go to school and to college to test nothing but memory. Then you pursue money, get a job and a car that you are still paying for, drive through traffic to the job you need so you can pay for the car and the house you leave all day to survive, start your own family, make some more money, and before you know it, you soon retire to await the end. But I tell you the truth, surely there is more to life than this vain rollercoaster.

For I tell you the truth, there comes a time in life where it falls upon a generation to be great, but the truth is a great generation is not one where your life is about surviving till you find the means to survive but no meaning to live for. Therefore I tell you the truth, I cannot deny the importance of one's deeds here on earth, for in the end, that is the true meaning we will find when we reach the end.

Let your life be filled with love like a child's; let your life be filled with joy like a child's; let your life be filled with unity like a child's; let your life be filled with imagination like a child's; let your life be filled with hope like a child's; let your life be filled with faith like a child's.

For I tell you the truth, we were all human beings
until religion separated us, race disconnected us,
politics divided us, and wealth classified us.

For I say to you, remember who you were before
the world told you who you are.

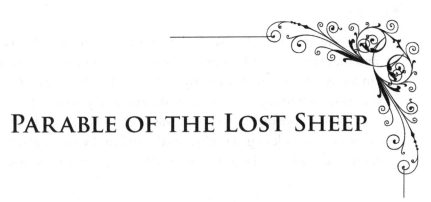

Parable of the Lost Sheep

See that you do not look down on one of these little ones. For I tell you that their angels in heaven always see the face of my Father in heaven. The Son of man came to save what was lost.

What do you think? If a man owns a hundred sheep, and one of them wanders away, will he not leave the ninety-nine on the hills and go to look for the one that wandered off? And if he finds it, I tell you the truth, he is happier about that one sheep than about the ninety-nine that did not wander off. In the same way, your Father in heaven is not willing that any of these little ones should be lost.

For I say to you, do not look down on any of your fellow man. For the truth is the Creator is within us all. For the Son of man came to show us that we were all made in the image of the Creator. For some people may have fooled all of the people some of the time, but I tell you the truth, they cannot fool all of the people all of the time.

For the truth is the time has come for each and every one who was once lost in hate to find love; the time for each and every one who was once lost in selfishness to find generosity; the time for each and every one who was once lost in sadness to find joy; the time for each and every one who was once lost in revenge to find forgiveness; the time for each and every one who was once lost in the world to find himself.

For just like a sheep, you may have wandered off. But I tell you the truth, the truth has come to set you free, to be free from injustice, to be free from hate, to be free from division, to be free from lack, to be free from fear, to be free from pain, and to be free to be your true self.

For I say to you, awake and find your way back to love. Awake and find your way back to peace. Awake and find your way back to joy. Awake and find your way back to unity. Awake and find your way back to righteousness. Awake and find your way back to forgiveness. Awake and find your way back to hope. Awake and find your way back to generosity. Awake and find your way back to faith, and I tell you the truth, you will find your way back home.

A Brother
Who Sins against You

If your brother sins against you, go and show him his fault, just between the two of you. If he listens to you, you have won your brother over. But if he will not listen, take one or take two others along, so that "every matter may be established by the testimony of two or three witnesses." If he refuses to listen to them, tell it to the court. And if he refuses to listen even to the court, treat him as you would a pagan or tax collector.

I tell you the truth, whatever you bind on earth will be bound in heaven, and whatever you loose on earth will be loosed in heaven. Again, I tell you that if two of you on earth agree about anything you ask for, it will be done for you by my father in heaven. For where two or three come together in my name, there am I with them.

> For the truth is if anyone has wronged you in this world,
> you ought to show them that they have wronged you,
> and if that person still will not treat you the way he ought
> to treat people, I say to you, let that person be.

For I tell you the truth, you will both not reach the conclusion
you seek. The truth is just because the Devil is being a devil does
not mean you should do evil. Just because a thief is being a thief
does not mean you should steal. Just because a criminal is being
a criminal does not mean you should be violent. Just because
a politician is lying does not mean you should be a liar. For I
say to you, let no man pull you low enough to hate them.

For the truth is you may not have control of how people behave, but you have control of how you respond. You may not have control of what people say to you, but you have control of what you say. You may not have control of the way people treat you, but you have control of how you treat them. You may not have control of world, but you have control of yourself.

For I tell you the truth, whatever you bind here on earth will be bound in heaven, and so whatever you loose on earth, will be loosed in heaven. For the truth is as it is heaven, so it will be earth; as it is within, so it will be without; as it is when it rises, so it will be when it falls.

For the truth is if you bind revenge within you, your world will be bound with revenge. If you bind hate within you, your world will be bound with hate. If you bind greed within you, your world will be bound with greed. If you bind evil within you, your world will be bound with evil. If you bind violence within you, your world will be bound with violence.

For I say to you, do not resist an evil person with evil. The truth is you will merely multiply the evil. Do not resist a violent person with violence; you will merely multiply the violence. Do not resist a greedy person with greed; you will merely multiply the greed. Do not resist a deceitful person with deceit. You will merely multiply the deceit. Do not resist a racist person with racism; you will merely multiply the racism. Do not resist a negative person with negativity; you will merely multiply the negativity.

For I tell you the truth, every way you respond to people comes from you; every way you respond to people is made up from you; and so every way you respond to people returns to you.

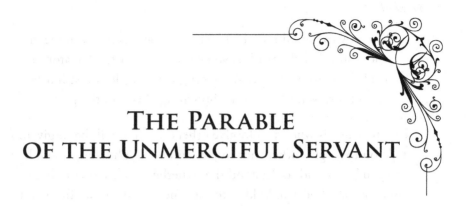

THE PARABLE
OF THE UNMERCIFUL SERVANT

Lord, how many times shall I forgive my brother when he sins against me?

Therefore, the kingdom of heaven is like a king who wanted to settle accounts with his servants. As he began the settlement, a man who owed him ten thousand talents was brought to him. Since he was not able to pay, the master ordered that he and his wife and his children and all that he had be sold to repay the debt. The servant fell on his knees before him. "Be patient with me," he begged, "and I will pay back everything." The servant's master took pity on him, cancelled the debt, and let him go. But when that servant went out, he found one of his fellow servants who owed him a hundred denarii. He grabbed him and began to choke him. "Pay back what you owe me!" he demanded.

His fellow servant fell to his knees and begged him, "Be patient with me, and I will pay you back." But he refused. Instead, he went and had the man thrown into prison until he could pay the debt.

When the other servants saw what had happened, they were greatly distressed and went and told their master everything that had happened. Then the master called the servant in. "You wicked servant," he said, "I cancelled all that debt of yours because you begged me to. Shouldn't you have had mercy on your fellow servant just as I had on you?"

In anger his master turned him over to the jailers to be tortured, until he should pay back all he owed. This is how my heavenly Father will treat each of you unless you forgive your brother from your heart.

For I say to you, do not be like the hypocrites that you see in the world. For the truth is you cannot expect the Creator to forgive you for your sins and wrongdoing while you still have not forgiven the person who wronged you in the past.

For the truth is when you forgive others, you too will be forgiven. I tell you to forgive others not so you will be a righteous person, but so you know and understand that whether you choose to forgive someone or choose to hold onto bitterness, it all comes from you. Whether you choose to forgive someone or choose to hold onto bitterness, it is all made up from you. Whether you choose to forgive someone or choose to hold onto bitterness, it will all return to you.

For I tell you the truth, as you cannot expect to pick an apple from an orange tree, you will not find forgiveness in a life of revenge. As you cannot expect to find roses from a sunflower, you will not find forgiveness in a life of bitterness. As you cannot expect to find gold in the sky, you will not find forgiveness in a life of deceit. As you cannot expect to find birds in the ocean, you will not find forgiveness in a life of evil.

For the truth is you must treat others in the very same way you wish to be treated. For whatever you hold in your heart will be what your life will become. Therefore I tell you the truth, if you want the Creator to forgive you, you too should forgive others for their wrongdoing.

For just as the king had forgiven the servant, the Creator will also forgive you. But I tell you the truth, just as the servant did not forgive his fellow servant, if you do not forgive your fellow human, the Creator will also not forgive you.

For I tell you the truth, every day is another chance to move from the dark and into the light of forgiveness. Do not spend your life being a prisoner while not seeing that you had the key all along.

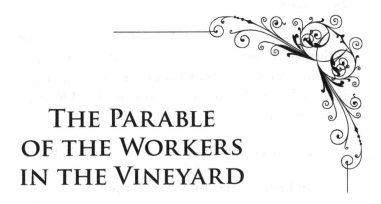

THE PARABLE
OF THE WORKERS
IN THE VINEYARD

For the kingdom of heaven is like a landowner who went out early in the morning to hire men to work in his vineyard. He agreed to pay them a denarius for the day and sent them into his vineyard. About the third hour he went out and saw others standing in the marketplace doing nothing. He told them, "You also go work in my vineyard, and I will pay you whatever is right." So they went. He went out again about the sixth hour and the ninth hour and did the same thing. About the eleventh hour he went out and found still others standing around. He asked them. "Why have you been standing here all day long doing nothing?"

"Because no one has hired us," they answered.

He said to them, "You also go and work in my vineyard."

When evening came, the owner of the vineyard said to his foreman, "Call the workers and pay them their wages, beginning with the last ones hired and going on to the first."

The workers who were hired about the eleventh hour came and each received a denarius. So when those came who were hired first, they expected to receive more, but each of them also received a denarius. When they received it, they began to grumble against the landowner. "These men who were hired last worked only one hour," they said, "and you have made them equal to us who have borne the burden of the work and the heat of the day."

But he answered one of them, "Friend, I am not being unfair to you. Didn't you agree to work for a denarius? Take your pay and go. I want to give the man who was hired last the same as I gave you. Don't I have the right to do what I want with my own money? Or are you envious because I am generous?"

So the last will be the first, and the first will be last.

For I tell you the truth, whoever you may be and wherever you
may be, you are unique, just like everyone else. You do not need
to be great to start, but you certainly need to start to be great.
Whatever you may have, empty pockets have never held anyone
back. Only empty hearts and empty heads do that. However
you may be, now is the best time to be how you want to be.

For I tell you the truth, the kingdom of heaven is always within
you at any time. Choosing to walk in the light will have the same
rewards no matter where you are. Choosing to walk in the light will
have the same rewards no matter who you are. Choosing to walk in
the light will have the same rewards whatever you have. Choosing
to walk in the light will have the same rewards however you may be.
Choosing to walk in the light will have the same rewards for us all.

For I say to you, do not walk in the darkness of envy while the light
within you still sparkles. Do not walk in the darkness of scarcity while
the light of abundance awaits everyone. Do not walk in the darkness
of selfishness while the light of generosity shines. Do not walk in the
darkness of greed while there is more than enough light for everyone.

For the truth is now is the time to start walking in the light whoever
you are. Now is the time to start walking in the light wherever you
are. Now is the time to start walking in the light whatever you have.
Now is the time to start walking in the light however you are.

For I tell you the truth, the Creator awaits you with all you
will ever need, want, or imagine. The door to the kingdom
of heaven opens with the key that is within you.

THE PARABLE
OF THE TWO SONS

What do you think? There was a man who had two sons. He went to the first and said, "Son, go and work today in the vineyard." "I will not," he answered, but later he changed his mind and went. Then the father went to the other Son and said the same thing. He answered, "I will sir," but he did not go. Which of the two did what his father wanted? "The first" they answered.

I tell you the truth, the tax collectors and the prostitutes are entering the kingdom of God ahead of you. For John came to you to show you the way of righteousness, and you did not believe him, but the tax collectors and the prostitutes did. And even after you saw this, you did not repent and believe him.

For I tell you the truth, through the eons that have come
to pass here on earth, there have been a few people like the
first son, who, when his father told him to go work in the
vineyard, at first refused but then later changed his mind.

For I tell you the truth, through the eons that have come to pass here
on earth, billions of people have been like the second son, who at first
promised his father that he would go work in the vineyard but never did.

For the truth is many of you were quick to proclaim that you will spend
you lives walking in the light of loving the Creator and loving others
as you would like to be loved yourself. But I tell you the truth, when
the time came for you to be righteous men and women, you chose to

ignore the Creator's commandments and spent your lives dedicated
to the pursuit of money and giving love only to those closest to you.

For I tell you the truth, the gate to the kingdom of heaven is
narrow, and only a few find it. Only a few people who were
not quick to claim that they are righteous, when the time
came for them to be righteous men and women, chose to
live a life dedicated to love and the service of others.

For I tell you the truth, you may have thought for a long time you were
doing what the Creator wanted by just saying you accepted the Son
of man as Lord and Saviour and you believe he rose from death after
three days. But I tell you the truth, you do what the Creator desires
only when you give love, only when you give hope, only when you give
peace, only when you give joy, and only when you give kindness.

For I tell you the truth, the deeds you do on earth carry a lot more
weight than the amount of scripture you quote. For I say to you, do
not make the mistake of being like the first son, who made a promise
that he knew he would not keep. For I tell you the truth, you will
see tax collectors and prostitutes enter the kingdom before you.

For I tell you the truth, the Son of man came and showed you the
way of righteousness, but still you did not turn from your ways.
Mother Teresa came and showed you the way of righteousness, but
still you did not turn from your ways. Martin Luther King came
and showed you the way of righteousness, but still you did not
turn from your ways. Nelson Mandela came and showed you the
way of righteousness, but still you did not turn from your ways.

For I tell you the truth, even after you saw many great men
and women walk the way of righteousness, you still chose
to walk in the darkness, but I tell you the truth, now is the
time to be the son that walks in the light of his Father.

SEVEN WOES

The teachers of the law and the Pharisees sit in Moses' seat. So you must obey them and do everything they tell you, but do not do what they do, for they do not practice what they preach. They tie up heavy loads and put them on men's shoulders, but they themselves are not willing to lift a finger to move them. Everything they do is done for men to see. They make their phylacteries wide and the tassels on their garments long. They love the place of honour at banquets and the most important seats in the synagogues. They love to be greeted in the marketplaces and to have men call them Rabbi.

But you are not to be called Rabbi, for you have only one master, and you are all brothers. And do not call anyone Father, for you have one Father, and he is in heaven. Nor are you to be called teacher, for you have one Teacher, the Christ. The greatest among you will be your servant. For whoever exalts himself will be humbled, and whoever humbles himself will be exalted.

Woe to you, teachers of the law and the Pharisees, you hypocrites! You shut the kingdom of heaven in men's faces. You yourselves do not enter, nor will you let those enter who are trying to. Woe to you, teachers of the law and Pharisees, you hypocrites! You devour widows' houses and for a show make lengthy prayers. Therefore you will be punished more severely.

Woe to you, teachers of the law and Pharisees, you hypocrites! You travel over land and sea to win a single convert, and when he becomes one, you make him twice as much a Son of hell as you are.

Woe to you, blind guides! You say, "If anyone swears by the temple, it means nothing, but if anyone swears by the gold of the temple, he is bound by his oath." You blind fools! Which is greater, the gold, or the temple that makes the gold sacred? You also say, "If anyone swears by the altar, it means nothing, but if anyone swears by the gift on it, he is bound by his oath." You blind men! Which is greater, the gift, or the altar that makes the gold sacred? Therefore, he who swears by the altar swears by it and by everything on it. And he who swears by the temple swears by it and by the one who dwells in it. And he who swears by heaven swears by God's throne and by the one who sits on it.

Woe to you, teachers of the law and Pharisees, you hypocrites! You give a tenth of your spices – mint, dill, and cumin, but you have neglected the more important matters of the law – justice, mercy, and faithfulness. You should have practiced the latter, without neglecting the former. You blind guides! You strain out a gnat but swallow a camel.

Woe to you, teachers of the law and Pharisees, you hypocrites! You clean the outside of the cup and dish, but inside they are full of greed and self-indulgence. Blind Pharisees! First clean the inside of the cup and dish, and then the outside will also be clean.

Woe to you, teachers of the law and Pharisees, you hypocrites! You are like whitewashed tombs, which look beautiful on the outside but on the inside are full of dead men's bones and everything unclean. In the same way, on the outside you appear to people as righteous, but on the inside you are full of hypocrisy and wickedness.

Woe to you, teachers of the law and Pharisees, you hypocrites! You build tombs for the prophets and decorate the graves of the righteous. And you say, "If we had lived in the days of our forefathers, we would not have taken part with them in shedding the blood of the prophets." So you testify against yourselves that you are the descendants of those who murdered the prophets. Fill up, then, the measure of the sin of your forefathers!

You snakes! You brood of vipers! How will you escape being condemned to hell? Therefore I am sending you prophets and wise men and teachers. Some of them you will kill and crucify; others you will flog in your synagogues and pursue from town to town. And so upon you will come all the righteous blood that has been shed on earth, from the blood of righteous Abel to the blood of Zechariah son of Be-rakiah, whom you murdered between the temple and the altar. I tell you the truth, all this will come upon this generation.

O Jerusalem, Jerusalem, you who kill the prophets and stone those sent to you, how often I have longed to gather your children together as a hen gathers her chicks under her wings. But you were not willing. Look, your house is left to you desolate. For I tell you, you will not see me again until you say, "Blessed is he who comes in the name of the Lord."

For I tell you the truth, the priests and the government sit in the seats of righteous men. They are the ones entrusted by the people to give direction and well-being to the nations.

I tell you the truth, you may listen to what they have to say, but I say to you, do not do what they do. For they place huge burdens and loads on people's backs while they themselves cannot lift even a finger to practice what they preach about.

For I tell you the truth, all they do is for people to see. On Sundays they preach in front of large crowds and tell the people to live a life of righteousness, but for the rest of the week, when it is time for them to practice what they preach, they are too busy being worried about the pursuit of money. Also, the governments will gather in front of crowds when it's time to vote, but I tell you the truth, when the time comes for them to deliver on their promises, they are too busy enjoying the thrills of the money and power they think they possess.

For I tell you the truth, they love the places of honour given to them by men and titles handed to them by the people. They love to be called by the names of honour given to them by the people and love being greeted and being called "Teacher" or "Father" by those who meet them at random places.

For I tell you the truth, you are not to call anyone "Teacher", for the truth is you have only one teacher, and that teacher is the Son of man.

93

For I tell you the truth, you are not to call anyone "Father", for the truth is you have only one father and that father is the Creator within you. For I tell you the truth, no man or woman is above another, for you are all brothers and sisters. All are but one part of a larger whole.

For the truth is the greatest amongst us is not the one given a position by the people. But I tell you the truth, the greatest amongst us is the one who is a servant to all. For whoever humbles himself will be exalted, and whoever exalts himself will be humbled.

For I tell you the truth, the priests and government are the very same people who killed the Son of man, for these men and women did exceptionally well at turning people into exactly the opposite of what was wanted. Their master plan to drag billions with them almost certainly worked like a woman spreading AIDS so she won't die alone. It's like they knew that the people will almost always choose what is easy and not right. They only had to open their legs like a Jezebel and the people rushed in without thinking. They gave birth to a world my Father didn't envision. Now soon He will return to a house in destruction, like a parent returning to find a party in his home. Oh, how I feel for those my Father will find dwelling joyfully, causing destruction. Now I cannot say Father forgive them, for they do not know what they doing because they knew all along.

For I tell you the truth, these men have shut the door to the kingdom of heaven for the people. They have made people think that the kingdom of heaven is accessible through the wide gate of quoting scripture and living a life to please others. They have made people think that they are angels who have come to lead them to the light. But I tell you the truth, they are wolves dressed up in large and shiny garments.

For I tell you the truth, these men and women are quick to clean the outside and neglect the inside. For the truth is the world has been dragged into the illusion of material things. It was more than easy for them to live clean lives outside where people witness their delusions as the truth, lives where they are righteous in front of people but in their hearts they are wicked. But I tell you the truth, as it is with a cup that is clean on the outside and dirty in the inside, when the time comes to drink up, it will be bitter when it's time to swallow.

For I tell you the truth, the Creator will send righteous men and women to grace this earth. These "leaders" of people have continued to belittle the deeds done by great and righteous men and women. They fool people by claiming that if they do not become part of their religion and movement, they can never enter the kingdom of the Creator. They are quick to forget that the Son of man had no religion, nor did the Creator. They are quick to forget that the Son of man did not just teach people the way of life by saying things. He also taught people the way of life by practicing what he preached.

For I tell you the truth, those that continue to lead the masses astray have made people believe that you cant expect them to be like the Son of man. But I tell you the truth: obviously, you can't walk on water; obviously, you can't heal the blind and sick; obviously, you can't wake up from the dead; obviously, you can't feed thousands with seven loaves; and obviously, you can't turn water in to wine. But I tell you the truth, there is certainly a thing or two that you can do. You can love like the Son of man; you can be generous like the Son of man; you can be peaceful like the Son of man; you can have hope like the Son of man; you can have faith like the Son of man; you can be joyful like the Son of man. For the truth is those things are not impossible. We both know that. Let us not fool ourselves and choose what is easy over what is right. Let us not sugar-coat things just so they benefit us!

Be careful not to be like those who clean the outside and neglect cleaning the inside. Don't clean the garden, outside walls, and yard just so others can see your cleanliness while neglecting the dirty kitchen, messy bedroom, and filthy lounge you alone sit in. Be careful not to make yourself beautiful on the outside with clothes, make-up, and material things while neglecting the quality of the thoughts, words, and actions that become your life.

For I tell you the truth, at this rate, according to those who lead the masses, 80 per cent of people are going to the kingdom of heaven because they have been saved. At this rate, according to the Son of man, 99 per cent are going to hell because none love their neighbours as they love themselves.

For I tell you the truth, we were all human beings until religion separated us. We were all human beings until race disconnected us. We were all human beings until politics divided us. And we were all human beings until wealth classified us.

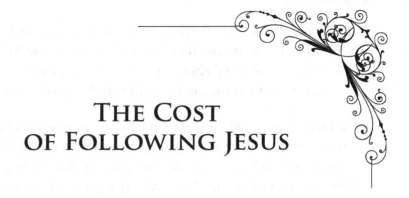

THE COST
OF FOLLOWING JESUS

If anyone of you wants to be my follower, you must turn from your selfish ways, take up your cross, and follow me. If you try to hang on to your life, you will lose it. But if you give up your life for my sake and for the sake of the good news, you will save it. And what do you benefit if you gain the whole world but lose your own soul? Is anything worth more than your soul? If anyone is ashamed of me and my message in these adulterous and sinful days, the Son of man will be ashamed of that person when he returns in the glory of his father with the holy angels.

For I tell you the truth, if you truly want to follow the Son of man, you should turn from the ways of the world; you should turn from the ways of hate; you should turn from the pursuit of money; you should turn from the ways of evil; you should turn from the pursuit of material things; you should turn from the ways of separation; you should turn from the ways of negativity; you should from the ways of scarcity.

For the truth is to truly follow the Son of man you should take up your life and follow the way of love; you should take up your life and follow the way of peace; you should take up your life and follow the way of generosity; you should take up your life and follow the way of faith; you should take up your life and follow the way of abundance; you should take up your life and follow the way to the kingdom of heaven.

For I tell you the truth, if you try to hang on to your life of selfish ways, selfish ways will come from you, selfish ways will be made up from you, and your selfish ways will return to you. If you try to hang on to your life of hate, the truth is the hate will always come from you, the hate will always be made up from you, and the hate will always return to you. If you try to hang on to your life of evil, the truth is the evil will always come from you, the evil will always be made up from you, and the evil will always return to you.

For I tell you the truth, if you try to hang on to your life of pursuing money and material things, you may gain the whole world and its treasures, which are here today and gone tomorrow, but you will lose your soul while still alive. And when you reach the end, when money and material things go to other people, when the body goes to the earth, and when the soul returns to the Creator, you will realize that no amount of money and material things is worth your soul.

For I tell you the truth, if you give up your life for the sake of love, you will not only gain love, but you will save your soul. If you give up your life for the sake of peace, you will not only gain peace, but you will save your soul. If you give up your life for the sake of joy, you will not only gain joy, but you will save your soul. If you give up your life for the sake of good, you will not only gain good, but you will save your soul. If you give up your life for the sake of the Son of man, you will not only gain heaven on earth, but you will save your soul.

For I tell you the truth, if you are ashamed of the message that I bring to you and the truth that I tell you, the Son of man will also be ashamed of you and the lies you listened to and lived by.

For the money and possessions go to other people, the body goes to the earth, and the soul goes the Creator.

RICHNESS

And I assure you that everyone who has given up house or brothers or sisters or mother or father or children or property, for my sake and for the sake of the good news, will receive now in return a hundred times as many houses, brothers, sisters, mothers, children, and property, along with persecution. And in the world to come that person will have eternal life. But many who are the greatest now will be least important then and those who seem least important now will be the greatest then.

If you have given up a house for the sake of good, I tell you the truth, you will gain much more than houses in the kingdom of heaven. If you have given up your mother or father for the sake of good, I tell you the truth, you will gain more mothers and fathers in the kingdom of heaven. If you have given up your brother or sister for the sake of good, I tell you the truth, you will gain more brothers and sisters in the kingdom of heaven. If you have given up property, I tell you the truth, you will gain more properties in the kingdom of heaven.

For I tell you the truth, if you choose to hang on to the life of money and material things, which may seem important for now, they will be less important later. If you choose to hang on to the temptations of the world, which are only exciting this moment and regretful the next, they will be less important later. If you choose to hang on to the life of greed, which may feel like having everything now, it will leave you feel like you have nothing later. If you choose to hang on to the life of the world, the world may seem important now, but the truth is your soul will be much more important then.

For I tell you the truth, those who may seem important now in the eyes of the world will be least important then. And I tell you the truth, those who are least important now will be the greatest then. For the truth is whatever was done in secret will be revealed; whoever did things for the sake of being seen will truly be seen; whatever things you did will be revealed.

For I tell you the truth, what may seem important now will be least important in the end. For the truth is the money and possessions go to other people, the body goes to the earth, and the soul goes to the Creator.

FIRST AND LAST

You know that the rulers in this world lord it over their people, and officials flaunt their authority over those under them. But among you it will be different. Whoever wants to be a leader among you must be your servant, and whoever wants to be a leader among you must be your servant, and whoever wants to be first among you must be the slave of everyone else. For even the Son of man came, not to be served, but to serve others and to give his life as a ransom for many.

For I tell you the truth, in this world you may have been classified by the amount of money you make; in this world you may have been separated by the religion you choose to be part of; in this world you may have been divided by the political parties you supported; and in this world you may have been disconnected by your race. But I tell you the truth, in the kingdom of the Creator there is no classification, there is no separation, there is no division, and there is no disconnection.

If you want to enter the kingdom of heaven and be a leader amongst men, I tell you the truth, you must first be the servant of others. If you want to enter the kingdom of heaven and be the first amongst men, I tell you the truth, you must be the slave of others.

For I tell you the truth, even the Son of man did not come to be served and worshiped. The truth is he came to serve and love others. For he gave his life to the service of others; he gave his life to the pursuit of good; he gave his life up to serve others.

For when he gave his life as a ransom for many, his life was dedicated to helping others and not dying for their sins. His life was dedicated to

giving love to others and not dying for their sins. His life was dedicated
to giving hope to others and not dying for their sins. His life was
dedicated to giving peace to others and not dying for their sins. His life
was dedicated to giving generously to others and not dying for their sins.

For I tell you the truth, the way to enter the kingdom of heaven
is through the Son of man. The way to the kingdom of heaven is
through serving others. The way to enter the kingdom of heaven
is through being a slave of everyone else. The way to enter the
kingdom of heaven is through giving your life as ransom for many.

PARABLE
OF THE TEN BRIDESMAIDS

Then the kingdom of heaven will be like ten bridesmaids who took their lamps and went to meet the bridegroom. Five of them were foolish, and five of them were wise. The five who were foolish didn't take enough olive oil for their lamps, but the other five were wise enough to take along extra oil. When the bridegroom was delayed, they all became drowsy and fell asleep.

At midnight they were roused by the shout, "Look, the bridegroom is coming! Come out and meet him!"

All the bridesmaids got up and prepared their lamps. Then the five foolish ones asked the others, "Please give us some of your oil because our lamps are going out."

But the others replied, "We do not have enough for all of us. Go to a shop and buy some for yourselves."

But while they were gone to buy oil, the bridegroom came. Then those who were ready went in with him to the marriage feast, and the door was locked. Later, when the other five bridesmaids returned, they stood outside, calling, "Lord! Lord! Open the door for us!"

But he called back, "Believe me, I don't know you!"

So you, too, must keep watch! For you do not know the day or the hour of my return.

For I tell you the truth, it has been about two thousand years since the Son of man graced the earth. The truth is some of you have been wise like the bridesmaids who took along enough olive oil for their lamps and have never walked away from the ways of love. But I tell you the truth, most of you have been foolish, like the bridesmaids who did not take along enough olive oil for their lamps and have neglected the ways of love and walked in the ways of the world.

For the truth is when the bridegroom was delayed and the bridesmaid became drowsy and feel asleep, so too have people become drowsy in the ways of the world and found themselves caught on a rollercoaster that they think will not end. For the truth is when the Son of man soon returns, they will be much more shocked than the bridesmaid who fell asleep during the wait, while others will be busy, caught in the pursuit of money and others caught in the ways of the world. And I tell you the truth, as there was no time for the foolish bridesmaids to go back and get more olive oil for their lamps, so too there will be no time for those who live according to the ways of the world.

For say to you, live your life with more than enough love, and you will have an abundance in the end. Live your life with more than enough peace, and you will always be prepaid for the Son of man. Live your life with more than enough joy, and you will have an abundance in the end. Live your life with more than enough forgiveness, and in the end the Son of man will have an abundance for you.

For I tell you the truth, you think going with the crowd is exciting and the true way for now, but you will never go further than the crowd. For the truth is you have to make sure that you bring enough love in the end so you do not get left behind. For the truth is if you do not know love, you do not know the Son of man.

Therefore, again I say to you, choose the way of love over the way of hate. Choose the way of peace over the way of violence. Choose the way of generosity over the way of greed. Choose the way of hope over the way of negativity. Choose the way of joy over the way of pain. Choose the way of the Son of man over the way of the world because I tell you the truth, you do not know the day or the hour of his arrival.

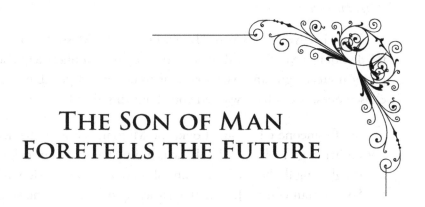

THE SON OF MAN
FORETELLS THE FUTURE

Do not let anyone deceive you, for many will come in my name, claiming, "I am the Messiah." They will deceive many, and you will hear of wars and threats of wars, but do not panic. Yes, these things must take place, but the end won't follow immediately. Nation will go to war against nation, and kingdom will go against kingdom. There will be famines and earthquakes in many parts of the world, but all this is only the first of the birth pains, with more to come.

Then you will be arrested, persecuted, and killed. You will be hated all over the world because you are my followers, and many will turn away from me and betray and hate each other. And many false prophets will appear and will deceive many people. Sin will be rampant everywhere, and the love of many will grow cold. But the one who endures to the end will be saved. And the good news about the kingdom will be preached throughout the whole world, so that all nations will hear it, and then the end will come.

The day is coming when you will see what Daniel the prophet spoke about – the sacrilegious object that causes desecration standing in the holy place. Then those in Judea must flee to the hills. A person out on the deck of a roof must not go down into the house to pack. A person out in the field must not return even to get a coat. How terrible it will be for pregnant women and nursing mothers in those days. And pray that your flight will not be in winter or on the sabbath. For there will be greater anguish than at any time since the world began, and it will never be so great again. In fact, unless that time of calamity is shortened, not a single person will survive, but it will be shortened for the sake of God's chosen ones.

Then if anyone tells you, "Look, here is the Messiah," or "There he is," do not believe it. For false messiahs and false prophets will rise up and perform great signs and wonders so as to deceive, if possible, even God's chosen ones. See, I have warned you about this ahead of time.

So if someone tells you, "Look, the Messiah is out in the desert," do not bother to go look. Or, "Look, he is hiding here," do not believe it! For as the lightning flashes in the east and shines to the west, so it will be when the Son of man comes. Just as the gathering of vultures shows there is a carcass nearby, so these signs indicate that the end is near.

Immediately after the anguish of those days, the sun will be darkened, the moon will give no light, the stars will fall from the sky, and the powers in the heavens will be shaken.

And then at last, the sign that the Son of man is coming will appear in the heavens, and there will be deep mourning among all the peoples of the earth. And they will see the Son of man coming on the clouds of heaven with power and great glory. And he will send out his angels with the mighty blast of a trumpet, and they will gather his chosen ones from all over the world, from the farthest ends of the earth and heaven.

Now learn a lesson from the fig tree. When its branches bud and its leaves begin to sprout, you know that summer is near. In the same way, when you see all these things, you can know his return is very near, right at the door. I tell you the truth, this generation will not pass from the scene until all these things take place. Heaven and earth will disappear, but my words will never disappear. However, no one knows the day or even the hour these things will happen, not even the angels in heaven or the Son himself. Only the father knows.

When the Son of man returns, it will be like it was in Noah's day. In those days before the flood, the people were enjoying banquets and parties and weddings right up to the time Noah entered his boat. People didn't realize what was going to happen until the flood came and swept them all away. That is the way it will be when the Son of man returns.

Two men will be working together in the field; one will be taken and the other left. Two women will be grinding flour at the mill; one will be taken and the other will be left.

So you too, must keep watch! For you do not know what day or hour your Lord is coming. Understand this: If a homeowner knew exactly when a burglar was coming, he would keep watch and not permit his house to be broken into. You also must be ready all the time, for the Son of man will come when least expected.

A faithful, sensible servant is one whom the master can give the responsibility of managing his other household servants and feeding them. If the master returns and finds that the servant has done a good job, there will be a reward. I tell you the truth, the master will put that servant in charge of all he owns. But what if the servant is evil and thinks, "My master will not be back for a while," and he begins beating the other servants, partying, and getting drunk? The master will return unannounced and unexpected, and he will cut the servant to pieces and assign him a place with the hypocrites. In that place there will be weeping and gnashing of teeth.

For I tell you the truth, you may have been deceived into thinking many different things about the Son of man. Many false prophets have risen to claim that they were sent by the Creator and have deceived many. You have heard of wars that are happening around the world. You have heard of earthquakes and famines that are happening around the world. You have heard of nations going against other nations around the world. You heard of brothers going against brothers around the world. But I tell you the truth, these things have come to pass so that the beginning of the end can happen.

For the truth is that while the world is full of sin, while the world is full of hate, while the world is full of greed, while the world is full of adultery, while the world is full of wars, while the world is full of division, while the world is full of negativity, many have turned away from the way of love, many have turned away from the way of unity, many have turned away from the way of peace, many have turned away from the way of generosity, many have turned away from the way of faith, many have turned away from the way of hope, many have turned away from the way of forgiveness, and so many have turned away from the way of the Son of man.

For I tell you the truth, if you endure with love till the end, you will be embraced and saved. If you endure with peace till the end, you will be free and saved. If you endure with generosity till the end, you will be rewarded and saved. If you endure with hope till the end, you will be delivered and saved. If you endure with faith till the end, you will be manifested and saved. For I have told you the truth about the kingdom of Creator, and the world will know the truth.

For I tell you the truth, in the end no one will be able to return to their house; in the end no one will be able to go get their money; in the end no one will be able to go get their clothes; in the end no one will be able to go get their car. For you may hear people claiming that they are the Son of man or that they see him, and you may see false prophets perform signs and wonders as they deceive many. But I tell you the truth: Now you know the truth before the end.

For I say to you if someone tells you, "Look, the Son of man is out in the desert," do not bother to go look. Or, "Look, the Son of man is hiding here," do not believe it! For as the lightning flashes in the east and shines to the west, so it will be when the Son of man comes. Just as the gathering of vultures shows there is a carcass nearby, so these signs indicate that the end is near.

For I tell you the truth, you should learn a lesson from the fig tree. When its branches bud and its leaves begin to sprout, you know that summer is near. In the same way, when you see all these things, you can know His return is very near, He is right at the door. For I tell you the truth, this generation will not pass from the scene until all these things take place. Heaven and earth will disappear, but the truth of these words will never disappear. However, no one knows the day or the hour these things will happen, not even the angels in heaven or the Son himself. Only the Creator knows.

For I tell you the truth, when the time for the end is upon us and the Son of man returns, many will be too busy in the pursuit of money, with others busy going to work and others at social events and parties. People will not realize the end has begun and will be in awe when the Son of man returns. While people are at work, one will be taken and one will be left. While people are at social events and parties, one will be taken and one will be left.

For I tell you the truth, you must always be prepared for the end, for you do not know the hour or the day the Creator will return. If you fail to prepare, I say to you, prepare to fail. For you already know the Creator will return. I say to you, await the end with your soul still intact.

For I tell you the truth, to be a faithful and wise servant of the Creator is to be one who can be trusted and given responsibility to care for the life that one is given, and to care for the life of others. For I tell you the truth, when the Creator returns, he will reward that faithful and wise servant.

An untrustworthy servant of the Creator is one who is trusted and given responsibility to care for the life that one is given and to care for lives of others. But I tell you the truth, that untrustworthy servant spends his life caring only for money and never caring for the lives of others. For I tell you the truth, when the Creator returns, he will punish that unfaithful and untrustworthy servant.

For I tell you the truth, I have learned that people trust insurance companies more than God. I have learned that people put more value on money than on a person's life. I have learned that people choose what is easy over what is right. I have learned that people would rather walk alone in the light than together in the dark. I have learned that people trust opinions more than their inner voices. I have learned that people cherish the visible, though the invisible creates the visible. Truly speaking, I have learned and learned, but still I know nothing.

ACKNOWLEDGEMENTS

Writing this book and the topic its all about was never going to be easy
for me, although many do not know this but it took all of me and I
had to lose all that I ever knew and loved. Through this book I have
not only risen to a calling but I have had a chance to tell the world of
its own purpose. I would like to thank my mother Maroloti Eunice
Makholwa for all the support she gave me when I needed it most and
the risks she took in making this book land in your hands. I would also
like to thank the whole Roloti (more specifically Phatheka, Phumla
and Kholi)and Makholwa families for their continued support through
me writing this book. To my sister's Nelly Makholwa Zondi, Bhedi
Makholwa Somtsai, Brenda Makholwa Mncwabe, Ayanda Makholwa
Tahwa and Xola Lithakazi Roloti as well as Miranda and Sisonke
Roloti I cannot put in words how you have inspired me to always
go a step further, and I can never thank you enough. To Mawande
Sibobi, Katlego More, Thulani Magubane, Yanga Roloti, Xabiso
Roloti, Okhanyo Roloti, Babalo Vuntu, Tsholofelo Puoeng, Romeo
Makofane thank you gentlemen for keeping me sane and the good
times and to Avela Mabetshe, i have no words but you understand.
To Sindiswa Magidla, Avela Macingwane, Zanda Ndima, and Boyka
Ntombela you may not know this but I have never had anyone believe
in me the way you did, and I would never have continued writing if it
wasn't for you, day and night I thank the Creator for the blessing you
are, it is because of people like you that I did not give up, you mean
the world to me. To Naledi Moagi, Noluthando Mnguni, Qhama
Zulu, Abulele Yako, Samukelisiwe Ndlovu, Zamangwana Malgas and
Paseka Mathathe I thank you for the invisible support you gave me. To
Tsholofelo Mofokeng thank you for pointing me in the right direction
when I started this book. To Luvo Disane our time walking the path of

truth, and sessions with invisible giants made me learn more than I ever been taught at school, if my path is cut short, you know what to do.

In as much as I have the above people to thank for the strength to write this book, the true inspiration and reason I wrote this book was because of these following giants I hold dear to my heart and as much as I cant wait to see you again, most of all I want to thank the man many know as Jesus, your teachings and life have elevated me to new heights and I hope through this book, your sacrifices were not in vain. To Martin Luther King junior, Albert Einstein, Michelangelo, Buddha, Mohamed, Mother Teresa, Mark Twain, Winston Churchill, Hellen Keller, Nelson Mandela, Mahatma Gandhi, Thomas Edison, Aristotle, Dr Sues, Alexandra Graham Bell, Maya Angelou, Isaac Newton, Plato, Henry Ford, Wright brothers, Socrates, Francis Bacon and many other righteous men and women who have graced this earth and walked in the light, I say to you my brothers and sisters, thank you. You have not only been the inspiration for me to wake up and continue your work, but your light is still shining in my path and through your teachings and lives I will bring your vision and dream for the future we all wanted to fruition. Again I say to you thank you, and I tell you the truth, I will see you on the other side.

NEW INTERNATIONAL VERSION

Matthew 5 ;
- Salt and light 13-16
- Fulfillment of the law 17-20
- Murder 21-26
- Adultery 27-30
- Divorce 31-32
- Oaths 33-37
- Eye for an eye 38-42
- Love for enemies 43-48

Matthew 6;
- Giving to the needy 1-4
- Prayer 5-15
- Treasures in heaven 19-24
- Do not worry 25-34

Matthew 7
- Judging others 1-6
- Ask, seek, knock 7-12
- Narrow and wide gates 13-14
- Tree and its fruit 15-23
- Wise and foolish builders 24-29

Matthew 13
- Parable of the sower 3-12 13-23
- Parables of the weeds 24-30
- Parables of the mustard seed and yeast 31-35
- Parable of the weeds explained 36-43

- Parable of hidden treasure and pearl 44-46
- Parable of the net 47-52

Matthew 18

- The greatest in the kingdom 1-9
- Lost sheep 10-14
- A brother who sins against you 15-20
- Unmerciful servant 21-35

Matthew 19

- Divorce 1-12

Matthew 20

- Parables of the workers in the vineyard 1-16
- Parables of the two sons 28-32
- Parables of the tenants 33-43

Matthew 22

- Parable of the wedding banquet 1-14

Matthew 23

- Seven woes 1-39

Matthew 24

- Signs of the end of the age 1-35
- The day and hour unknown 36-51

Matthew 25

- Parable of the ten virgins/ bridesmaid 1-13
- Parables of the talents 14-30
- Sheep and the goats 31-46

Printed in the United States
By Bookmasters

Printed in the United States
By Bookmasters